ON SERVANTHOOD AND REPENTANCE

‘Ubayd Allāh al-Samarqandī
(d. 701/1301)

On Servanthood and Repentance

A Critical Edition and Annotated Translation
by
Lejla Demiri

CMC PRESS

First published 2023 by

CMC Press
14 St Paul's Road
Cambridge CB1 2EZ
United Kingdom

ISBN 978-1-916608-00-9

Printed in Turkey

Table of Contents

Note on Transliteration and Dates vii
Introduction 1
Critical Edition & Annotated Translation 11
Risālat al-'Ubūdiyya, 'Treatise on Servanthood' 13
Risālat al-Tawba, 'Treatise on Repentance' 47
Bibliography 89
Index of Qur'anic Verses 93
Index of Hadith 97
Index 101

Note on Transliteration and Dates

The transliteration of Arabic names follows that of *The Encyclopaedia of Islam THREE (EI^3)*. Technical terms in Arabic are all italicised except for terms that have become common in English (e.g. Hadith, Islam, imam, mufti, sufi, Sunni, Shi'i). The *tā' marbūṭa* (ـة/ة) is rendered as 'a' (e.g. sūra), or as 'at' when the word is in the construct state (*iḍāfa*) (e.g. Sūrat al-Fātiḥa). Double dates are used in reference to the Islamic (A.H.) and Common Era (C.E.) calendars (e.g. 716/1316).

Introduction

Considering Ash'arism and Māturīdism, two of the major theological schools of Sunni Islam, a considerable amount of academic work exists on the former, with relatively scant attention paid to the latter. Similarly, contemporary Muslim knowledge of the Māturīdī tradition is significantly narrow and remains confined to a few books and authors whose names are still only superficially known. However, in recent years, a growing interest in Māturīdī theology has led to a significant increase in scholarly literature.[1]

With the intention to make Māturīdī literature more widely accessible and to contribute towards a better understanding of this rich scholarly tradition, the present study aims to present two short treatises by a Ḥanafī and Māturīdī scholar who was active in 13th century Damascus: Abū Muḥammad al-Bārsāh Rukn al-Dīn 'Ubayd Allāh ibn Muḥammad ibn 'Abd al-'Azīz al-Samarqandī (d. 701/1301). As indicated by his *nisba*, 'Ubayd Allāh al-Samarqandī was originally from Samarqand (ostensibly born around mid- 7th/13th century); he studied in Baghdad and then moved to Damascus where he spent the last ten years of his life. He taught in various mosques of Damascus and at the famous Ẓāhiriyya madrasa; had a teaching circle in the Umayyad Mosque, and was later appointed as *mudarris* or lecturer at the Nūriyya madrasa. A few days after his last appointment his dead body was found at the Ẓāhiriyya madrasa, and as it turned out, he had been murdered by a porter of the school, the circumstances of which are not articulated in biographical sources.[2]

1 For an overview of the current state of scholarship on Māturīdī thought, in various languages, see Dale J. Correa, "An Overview of the Current Scholarship on Māturīdī *Kalām* in Arabic, Persian and European Languages", *Māturīdī Theology. A Bilingual Reader*, ed. Lejla Demiri, Philip Dorroll and Dale J. Correa, Tübingen: Mohr Siebeck, 2022, pp. 3-13; Philip Dorroll, "Māturīdī Studies in Turkish. Historical Outline and Main Contributions", *Māturīdī Theology. A Bilingual Reader*, pp. 15-24.

2 For his life and work, see Mustafa Sinanoğlu, "Semerkandî, Ubeydullah b. Muhammed", *Türkiye Diyanet Vakfı İslam Ansiklopedisi*, Ankara: Türkiye Diyanet Vakfı, 2009, vol. 36, pp. 480-1.

Not much about Samarqandī's biography is known, although he was considered one of the major scholars of the Ḥanafī-Māturīdī tradition at the time.[3] He hence followed the Ḥanafī *madhhab* in law and the Māturīdī school in theology.[4] Coming from the rich scholarly tradition of the *'ulamā'* of *Mā warā' al-nahr* or Transoxiana,[5] with his numerous works Samarqandī contributed to various disciplines of Islamic learning, including *kalām*, *fiqh*, *tafsīr*, *ḥadīth* and *taṣawwuf*. As a prolific author he left a rich body of textual material behind, and yet he is almost unknown in the modern scholarship of Islam. Only two of his books, one in doctrine, his *'aqīda*,[6] and one in

3 See, for instance, Ṣalāḥ al-Dīn Khalīl ibn Aybak al-Ṣafadī, *Kitāb al-Wāfī bi-l-wafayāt*, ed. Aḥmad al-Arnā'ūṭ and Turkī Muṣṭafā, Beirut: Dār Iḥyā' al-Turāth al-'Arabī, 1420/2000, vol. 19, pp. 271-2; idem, *A'yān al-'aṣr wa-a'wān al-naṣr*, ed. 'Alī Abū Zayd et al., Beirut: Dār al-Fikr al-Mu'āṣir, 1418/1998, vol. 3, pp. 207-8; Ibn Ḥajar al-'Asqalānī, *al-Durar al-kāmina fī a'yān al-mi'a al-thāmina*, Beirut: Dār al-Jīl, 1931, vol. 2, p. 433; Abū l-Maḥāsin Jamāl al-Dīn Yūsuf ibn Taghribardī, *al-Dalīl al-shāfī 'alā l-manhal al-ṣāfī*, ed. Fahīm Muḥammad Shaltūt, Mecca: Jāmi'at Umm al-Qurā, [1980], vol. 1, p. 437.

4 The Māturīdiyya considers itself to represent the doctrine of Abū Ḥanīfa (d. 150/767). Abū Manṣūr Muḥammad al-Māturīdī (d. 333/944), traditionally viewed as the founder of the school, identified himself as a follower of Abū Ḥanīfa both in matters of *kalām* and *fiqh*. See Yusuf Şevki Yavuz, "Mâtürîdiyye", *Türkiye Diyanet Vakfı İslam Ansiklopedisi*, Ankara: Türkiye Diyanet Vakfı, 2003, vol. 28, pp. 165-75, at p. 165.

5 An ancient region in Central Asia, which corresponds to modern day Uzbekistan, Tajikistan and southwest Kazakhstan. After its spread throughout Central Asia, in the middle of the 11th century, Māturīdism expanded into the central Islamic world, throughout western Persia, Iraq, Anatolia, Syria and Egypt. Numerous Ḥanafī scholars from Central Asia migrated to these regions and taught there. Māturīdī doctrine thus gradually came to prevail among these Ḥanafī communities (W. Madelung, "Māturīdiyya", *Encyclopaedia of Islam. Second Edition*, ed. P. Bearman, Th. Bianquis, C.E. Bosworth, E. van Donzel, W.P. Heinrichs, Leiden: Brill, 1991, vol. 6, pp. 847-8, at p. 847). Māturīdism continued to spread further westwards as well as eastwards. The Ḥanafīs of Samarqand played an important role in the formation of the Ottoman intellectual tradition in Anatolia as well as Rumelia. They were further instrumental in spreading Islam into India, western China and Southeast Asia (the Indo-Malay world). See Philipp Bruckmayr, "The Spread and Persistence of Māturīdī Kalām and Underlying Dynamics", *Iran and the Caucasus*, 13 (2009), pp. 59-92.

6 Rukn al-Dīn 'Ubayd Allāh ibn Muḥammad al-Samarqandī, *al-'Aqīda al-rukniyya fī sharḥ lā ilāha ill Allāh Muḥammad Rasūl Allāh*, ed. Mustafa Sinanoğlu, Istanbul: İSAM, 2008.

uṣūl al-fiqh comparing Ḥanafī and Shāfiʿī principles of jurisprudence,[7] have been recently published in Turkey, each including a short analysis of the relevant text. None of his other writings (which are preserved in manuscripts in the libraries of Istanbul, Bursa and Kastamonu) seem to have been published or attracted any scholarly attention. In Turkish there exist two very short encyclopedia entries, one on his life[8] and another on his *ʿaqīda*;[9] and in English his *ʿaqīda* is briefly described in a recent publication,[10] and more recently a selection of his *ʿaqīda* is presented and translated with an annotation.[11] Except for these publications, to my knowledge, to date there exists no other study about him or his scholarly legacy.

What makes Samarqandī's theology so interesting for us today is that he is not a dry theologian, *mutakallim*, or dialectician; rather his *kalām* is combined with his sufi ideas, learnings and spirituality. One may compare him to Abū Ḥāmid al-Ghazālī (d. 505/1111), a follower of Ashʿarī tradition who was able to merge theology with sufi metaphysics. Just as in the writings of Ghazālī, in Samarqandī's works we find numerous *kalām* scholars mentioned and quoted side by side with various sufi authorities. In Samarqandī's *ʿAqīda*, both Ghazālī[12] and his brother Aḥmad al-Ghazālī (d. 520/1126) feature[13] alongside other Ashʿarīs such as Abū l-Ḥasan al-Ashʿarī (d. 324/936),[14] and Fakhr al-Dīn al-Rāzī (d. 606/1210).[15] As for Ḥanafī-Māturīdī sources, one would notice Abū Ḥanīfa (d. 150/767),[16]

7 Rukn al-Dīn ʿUbayd Allāh ibn Muḥammad al-Samarqandī, *Jāmiʿ al-uṣūl fī bayān al-qawāʿid al-ḥanafiyya wa-l-shāfiʿiyya fī uṣūl al-fiqh*, ed. İsmet Garibullah Şimşek, Istanbul: İSAM, 2020, 2 vols.

8 Sinanoğlu, "Semerkandî, Ubeydullah b. Muhammed", pp. 480-1.

9 Yusuf Şevki Yavuz, "el-ʿAkîdetü'z-Zekiyye" [sic], *Türkiye Diyanet Vakfı İslam Ansiklopedisi*, Ankara: Türkiye Diyanet Vakfı, 1989, vol. 2, pp. 260-1.

10 Gibril Fouad Haddad, *The Maturidi School from Abu Hanifa to al-Kawthari*, Oldham: Beacon Books, 2021, pp. 101-8.

11 Lejla Demiri, "God and Creation. ʿUbayd Allāh al-Samarqandī (d. 701/1301), *al-ʿAqīda al-rukniyya fī sharḥ lā ilāha ill Allāh Muḥammad Rasūl Allāh*", *Māturīdī Theology. A Bilingual Reader*, ed. Lejla Demiri, Philip Dorroll and Dale J. Correa, Tübingen: Mohr Siebeck, 2022, pp. 89-102.

12 Samarqandī, *al-ʿAqīda al-rukniyya*, pp. 54-6.

13 Ibid., p. 56.

14 Ibid., p. 76.

15 Ibid., pp. 71, 76.

16 Ibid., pp. 87, 117, 140.

Abū Manṣūr al-Māturīdī (d. 333/944),[17] Abū l-Layth al-Samarqandī (d. 373/983),[18] Muḥammad ibn Yaḥyā al-Bushāghirī (c. 4th/10th century), Abū Zayd al-Dabbūsī (d. 430/1039),[19] Shams al-A'imma Abū Bakr al-Sarakhsī (d. 483/1090),[20] and Abū l-Yusr al-Bazdawī (d. 493/1100).[21] Samarqandī does not hesitate to cite from the scholarly literature of different theological schools including Mu'tazilites,[22] Ḥanbalites,[23] or philosophers[24] such as Ibn Sīnā (d. 428/1037),[25] and sufis.[26] He equally draws his inspiration from Ash'arī and Māturīdī sources, blending them with those of sufis of diverse *mashrabs* or spiritual dispositions, such as al-Junayd al-Baghdādī (d. 298/911),[27] Abū Bakr al-Kalābādhī al-Bukhārī (d. 380/990),[28] Abū Ṭālib al-Makkī (d. 386/996),[29] and Shihāb al-Dīn al-Suhrawardī (d. 587/1191).[30]

The present book includes a critical edition and an annotated translation of two short treatises by Samarqandī, which have never been published before: (1) *Risālat al-'Ubūdiyya*, 'Treatise on Servanthood' and (2) *Risālat al-Tawba*, 'Treatise on Repentance'. Here the contents of the two treatises will be introduced, followed by a short description of the existing manuscripts, critical edition and annotated translation of each *risāla*.

In both treatises, Samarqandī's sources of reference are primarily the Qur'an and Hadith, alongside quotations from scholarly figures, such as Muḥammad ibn Yaḥyā al-Bushāghirī (c. 4th/10th century) and Abū l-Qāsim al-Shahīd al-Samarqandī (d. 556/1161) from among the early Māturīdī theological circles, and the famous Ash'arī theologian Fakhr al-Dīn al-Rāzī (d. 606/1210). He also frequently includes citations or stories from early sufi

17 Ibid., p. 69.
18 Ibid., pp. 70, 109.
19 Ibid., p. 72.
20 Ibid., p. 72.
21 Ibid., p. 72.
22 See, for instance, ibid., pp. 52, 66, 68, 71, 75, 78, 79, 81, 90, 92, 100, 114, 116, 122, 125, 126, 133, 135.
23 Ibid., pp. 67-8.
24 See ibid., pp. 54-5, 100, 114, 126, 133, 135, 136.
25 Ibid., p. 74.
26 See, for instance, his reference to *al-muḥaqqiqūn min al-ṣūfiyya*, ibid., p. 70.
27 Ibid., pp. 86, 91.
28 Ibid., pp. 108-9.
29 Ibid., p. 115.
30 Ibid., p. 123.

figures, some mentioned anonymously and some by name, such as ʿAbd Allāh ibn al-Mubārak (d. 118/736 or 181/797), Dhū l-Nūn al-Miṣrī (d. c. 245/859), Abū ʿAlī al-Warrāq (d. c. 3rd/9th century), Abū Yazīd al-Bisṭāmī (d. 261/874-5 or 234/848-9), Abū Ḥafṣ al-Ḥaddād (d. c. 265/878-90), al-Junayd al-Baghdādī (d. 298/911), Abū Bakr al-Wāsiṭī (d. c. 320/932), Muḥammad ibn Khafīf al-Shīrāzī (d. 371/982), Abū Bakr al-Kalābādhī al-Bukhārī (d. 380/990), and Shihāb al-Dīn al-Suhrawardī (d. 587/1191).

It is noteworthy that our author does not present his views about servanthood or repentance as exclusively the fruit of the Māturīdī milieu. Overall, he considers his position to be that of the *Ahl al-Sunna* (People of the Sunna), which he on two occasions explicitly mentions when contrasting the Sunni position with that of the Muʿtazila. This particularly relates to the question of whether one's repenting for some sinful acts without repenting for certain others is valid. According to the *Ahl al-Sunna*, Samarqandī writes, such a repentance is valid, while according to the Muʿtazila it is not.[31] Samarqandī's use of the category of *Ahl al-Sunna* is surely not limited to the Māturīdīs here, as this position is also held by the Ashʿarīs. One such example is a citation in a lengthy *kalām* summa attributed to Fakhr al-Dīn al-Rāzī;[32] while prior to Razī the same opinion is also mentioned by his father Ḍiyāʾ al-Dīn al-Makkī (d. 559/1163-65) as well as the latter's teacher Abū l-Qāsim al-Anṣārī (d. 512/1118), the most important student of Abū l-Maʿālī al-Juwaynī (d. 478/1085).[33] Samarqandī's two works presented here, therefore, exemplify the way in which a 13th century Māturīdī-Ḥanafī scholar, of Transoxianan origin, residing in a diverse Damascene scholarly setting, articulates his theological opinions within the broader spectrum of Sunni tradition. One may further argue that themes relevant to practical theology such as servanthood or repentance may not necessarily generate

31 ʿUbayd Allāh al-Samarqandī, *Risālat al-Tawba*, ed. Lejla Demiri (present edition), §§ 5 and 19.

32 This is a still unpublished work, entitled *Kitāb Uṣūl al-dīn ʿaqāʾid ahl al-sunna*, which, according to Ayman Shihadeh, is the earliest extant theological work authored by Rāzī. See Ayman Shihadeh, "Al-Rāzī's Earliest *Kalām* Work. Eastern Ashʿarism in the Twelfth Century", *Philosophical Theology in Islam. Later Ashʿarism East and West*, ed. Ayman Shihadeh & Jan Thiele, Leiden: Brill, 2019, pp. 36-70. For a citation from Rāzī's work, particularly the passages dealing with repentance for some sins without repentance for certain others, see ibid., pp. 52-3.

33 See ibid., p. 54.

a platform for the firm promotion of one's doctrinal positionalities. Hence the absence of an advocacy for a specific school of theology in Samarqandī's two treatises, which are written in the form of guidebooks for guiding and instructing the reader in the spiritual life. This defers, we may note, to the style of his contemporary Ibn Taymiyya (d. 728/1328), the Ḥanbalī scholar of Damascus, who although he uses his own treatise, which carries the same title *Risālat al-ʿUbūdiyya*,[34] as an occasion for criticizing certain opposing positions,[35] nonetheless provides a criticism less severe than that customarily found in his other writings.

As the title suggests, Samarqandī's *Risālat al-ʿUbūdiyya*, 'Treatise on Servanthood', is dedicated to exploring the duties of the *ʿabd*, servant of God, and his/her relationship with the *Maʿbūd*, the Worshipped One. Samarqandī opens the treatise with a definition of servanthood, which he defines as 'freedom'. Becoming a servant of God sets one free from becoming a slave of anyone or anything else. He introduces three degrees of such servanthood, all of which come from the same root of *ʿ-b-d*, to serve or worship. These are: (1) *ʿibāda* or worship of God with one's body; (2) *ʿubūdiyya* or servanthood of God with one's heart; and (3) *ʿubūda* or servitude of God with one's spirit. Each of these he relates to a familiar threefold categorisation of certainty: (1) *ʿilm al-yaqīn* – corresponding to serving God with one's body; (2) *ʿayn al-yaqīn* – achieved by serving God with one's heart; and (3) *ḥaqq al-yaqīn* – the highest degree of certainty that corresponds to Samarqandī's *ʿubūda*, i.e. serving God with one's spirit.[36]

Throughout the treatise, Samarqandī often reminds the reader that servanthood is about lowliness (*tadhallul*) and humility (*tawāḍuʿ*) before the Creator, and stands in stark contrast with arrogance (*takabbur*) which ultimately leads one to *shirk* or polytheism.[37] In support of his reflections,

34 Ibn Taymiyya, *Epistle on Worship. Risālat Al-ʿUbūdiyya*, trans. James Pavlin, Cambridge: Islamic Texts Society, 2015. The work itself does not provide any information as to when it was written. Its translator suggests that 'it was most likely written' during Ibn Taymiyya's time in Egypt or shortly after (ibid., p. xciv), which would place it long after the death of Samarqandī in 701/1301.

35 See especially his discussions on predestination and free will (ibid., pp. 9-12, 16-26) and his criticism of antinomianism (ibid., pp. 15, 65, 70-81).

36 ʿUbayd Allāh al-Samarqandī, *Risālat al-ʿUbūdiyya*, ed. Lejla Demiri (present edition), § 3.

37 See, for instance, ibid., § 4.

Samarqandī provides numerous quotations from various early sufi masters.[38] He then lists six different types of worship, which may involve primarily the individuals, their bodies or finances, as well as those which comprise merely collective duties.[39] This is then followed by a section on calamities which may compromise worship. Here he speaks of three such dangers: (1) languor (*fatra*), (2) love of praise (*ḥubb al-madḥ*), and (3) conceit (*ʿujb*). He thus underlines the crucial importance of consistency in worship, and warns us from the dangers of ostentation and self-praise, which he repeatedly identifies as forms of hidden idolatry.[40]

Finally the treatise concludes with a short section on integrity (*istiqāma*) and its relevance to one's servanthood. *Istiqāma* is defined as finding and maintaining due balance between excess (*ifrāṭ*) and inadequacy (*tafrīṭ*).[41] It is noteworthy that the treatise ends on this note of balance, which in a way summarizes the overall theme of the work. The message is clear: that as well as the balance between inward and outward, there exists the balance between body, mind and spirit, and also the balance between doing too much and doing too little.

Having thus laid out the duties of the servant of God, in his *Risālat al-Tawba*, 'Treatise on Repentance', Samarqandī explores the ways of finding reconciliation when the *ʿabd* (servant/worshipper) fails to fulfil her/his promise to the *Maʿbūd* (Worshipped). He begins with emphasizing the importance of repentance, which he considers as the very foundation of wayfaring. It is through repentance that one enters the spiritual journey to God.[42] He speaks of five different types of repentance, corresponding to five degrees of human perfection. The nearer one is to God the more scrupulous one's understanding of what constitutes a wrong act for which one has to repent.[43] Different types of *tawba* will be subsequently listed under three categories: *tawba* (turning away from sin), *awba* (turning one's attention from the blessing itself to the Bestower of the blessing), and *ināba* (turning away from anything other than God).[44]

38 Ibid., §§ 6-18.
39 Ibid., § 21.
40 Ibid., § 23.
41 Ibid., § 24.
42 Samarqandī, *Risālat al-Tawba*, § 2.
43 Ibid., § 6.
44 Ibid., § 14.

For Samarqandī, repentance begins by acknowledging the abhorrent nature of the sin,[45] which is then followed by three matters which constitute the very essence of repentance: (1) regret for the sinful act; (2) desisting from the error; and (3) determination to refrain from it in the future. He also mentions three other qualities which are required for one's repentance to be complete, though they are not considered to be part of repentance: (1) obtaining forgiveness from those one has wronged against; (2) making up what has been neglected; and (3) purifying the heart from past transgressions.[46]

Samarqandī urges his reader to rush into repentance, even if one were to return to the sinful act again and again. The very thought that 'there is no use in repentance if one cannot keep it', is actually from Satan and should not be heeded. Samarqandī reads the Qur'anic message, 'God loves those who turn to Him in repentance (*tawwābīn*)' (Q 2:222), as an indication that God wants us to be persistent in our repentance no matter how often we break it by going back to the sinful act. For the designation of *tawwāb* in this verse applies only to those who frequently repent.[47] This is the *tawba* of the servant. However, Samarqandī notes, *tawba* is also an attribute of God, which indicates firstly that God facilitates repentance for His servants by guiding them to repent, secondly that He makes them firm in their repentance, and thirdly that He accepts their repentance. So, even the turning of the sinner to God (human *tawba*) is a divine act and mercy, and is encompassed within God's turning to the servant (divine *tawba*).[48]

Samarqandī further reflects on the difference between regret and repentance,[49] as well as the difference between the believing sinner's repentance and that of the unbeliever.[50] Just as in his 'Treatise on Servanthood', here also Samarqandī underlines the importance of integrity (*istiqāma*) when he speaks about the repentance of integrity (*tawbat al-istiqāma*), which he finds to be the most difficult kind of repentance. It is to guard against excessiveness (*ifrāṭ*) and deficiency (*tafrīṭ*) in one's inner life and to seek forgiveness for whatever excessive or deficient things may have occurred throughout life. Keeping firmly to the middle way is extremely challenging and therefore,

45 Ibid., § 16.
46 Ibid., § 7.
47 Ibid., § 12.
48 Ibid., § 15.
49 Ibid., § 17.
50 Ibid., §§ 20-22.

Samarqandī notes, we are commanded to pray and ask for integrity in the opening of the Qur'an: 'Guide us to the straight path' (Q 1:6), in the sūra Fātiḥa which we are enjoined to recite in every prayer.[51]

Having underlined the importance of being ceaselessly preoccupied with repentance as one traverses one's spiritual path,[52] Samarqandī then turns our attention to the way to treat others around us who commit sin and repent. His message is clear: 'It is impermissible to upbraid and scold those who commit many errors [or those who constantly commit errors]'.[53] Likewise, reproaching someone after their repentance is not permitted.[54]

He then completes his treatise by mentioning some signs that indicate that repentance is accepted,[55] and offering some suggestions to a sincere repentant: to abandon temptations, to avoid mingling with people of temptation, and to guard against entertaining any thoughts of transgressions lest this incite the soul to commit them. Instead, one should mix with people of goodness and piety, and listen, read and reflect on aphorisms and exhortations as well as stories of the righteous ones and consider truthful thoughts. All of this will help one to habituate oneself to goodness. For, Samarqandī concludes, 'good is a habit and evil is a habit, and the soul is habituated; whatever you habituate it to, it will be habituated with that thing.'[56] Samarqandī closes his treatise with this important note that the human being is a creature of habit, making the task of training the soul to be paramount, since no one is evil by nature. Hence the importance of repentance, which is to be turned into a continuous habit.

51 Ibid., §§ 23-24.
52 Ibid., §§ 25-27.
53 Ibid., § 28.
54 Ibid., § 29.
55 Ibid., § 30.
56 Ibid., § 31.

Critical Edition
&
Annotated Translation

Risālat al-'Ubūdiyya
'Treatise on Servanthood'

The present edition is based on the three existing manuscripts of 'Ubayd Allāh al-Samarqandī's *Risālat al-'Ubūdiyya*, 'Treatise on Servanthood':

أ	MS Istanbul, Süleymaniye – Esad Efendi 1695, fols. 91b-93a (undated).
ب	MS Bursa, Bölge Yazmalar Ktp. – Ulucami 1674, fols. 44a-51b (completed on 5 Jumādā l-ākhir 705 / 23 December 1305).
ح	MS Istanbul, Süleymaniye – Hacı Beşir Ağa 387, fols. 116a-120a (undated).

MS Esad Efendi and MS Ulucami are very similar, but the latter (Ulucami) seems to be more accurate and presumably older than the former (Esad Efendi). MS Hacı Beşir Ağa includes frequent mistakes (misreadings); passages are often omitted or misplaced.

Abbreviations:

و	Folio recto
ظ	Folio verso
هـ	Margins of a given manuscript
–	Word/s absent in the manuscript
+	Additional word/s present in the manuscript
[ ]	Word/s added to the text by the editor

رسالة العبودية

Treatise on Servanthood

[أ ٩١ظ || ب ٤٤و || ح ١١٦ظ]

بسم الله الرحمن الرحيم[١]

{١} الحمد لله الذي أدرَّ[٢] عِهادَ[٣] لطائفِه على أهل العبادة إحساناً، وأسال شِعابَ[٤] مزيد عوارفِه على أهل العبوديّة فضلاً وامتناناً[٥]، وأفاض شآبيب[٦] لطائفه على أهل العبودة[٧]، وآمَنَهم عن ذُلِّ الحجاب إيماناً[٨]، ونشهد أن لا إله إلاّ الله وحده لا شريك له تسليماً وإيماناً[٩]، ونشهد أنّ محمّداً[١٠] عبده ورسوله أرْسِلَ إلى الخلق لينالوا به اهتداءً وإيقاناً[١١]، صلّى الله عليه[١٢] وعلى عِتْرَتِه[١٣] وصحبه[١٤] ما ذرَّ[١٥] شارقٌ[١٦] ولَمَعَ بارقٌ[١٧].

١ ح + وبه نستعين؛ ب + رسالة أخرى في العبادة والعبودية.
٢ ح: أمطر.
٣ ب هـ: العَهْدُ المطر يكون بعد المطر والجمع العِهادُ والعُهُودُ. من **الصحاح**.
٤ ب هـ: الشِّعَبُ بالكسر الطريق في الجبل والجمع الشِّعاب.
٥ ح: وإنعاما.
٦ ب هـ: الشؤبُوبُ الدُّفعَةُ من المطر وغيره والجمع الشَّآبِيبُ الدُّفعَةُ المطر مثلَ الدفعَة وهي المَرَّةُ الواحِدة العارفة المعروف. من **الصحاح**.
٧ أ: العبودية.
٨ ح – وأفاض شبائب لطائفه على أهل العبودة وآمنهم عن ذلّ الحجاب إيماناً.
٩ ح – تسليماً وإيماناً.
١٠ ح + عليه السلام.
١١ ح – أرسل إلى الخلق لينالوا به اهتداءً وإيقاناً.
١٢ ح – صلى الله عليه.
١٣ ح: آله.
١٤ ح: وصحنه.
١٥ ب هـ: ذرَّت تَذُرُّ ذُرُوراً طلعَتْ ويقال ذرَّ النَفْلُ إذا أطلَعَ من الأرض.
١٦ ب هـ: الشارق الشمس. من **الصحاح**.
١٧ ح – ما ذرَّ شارق ولمع بارق.

In the name of God, the Most Merciful, the Compassionate

{1} Praised be God, Who out of kindness makes the continuous rain of His beneficences flow abundantly upon the people of worship (*ahl al-ʿibāda*), causes the watercourse of His increased bounties to stream upon the people of servanthood (*ahl al-ʿubūdiyya*) as a free gift and favour, and floods the downpour of His subtle graces over the people of servitude (*ahl al-ʿubūda*)[1] and renders them truly safe from the lowliness of veiling. In true submission and faith, we bear witness that there is no god except God, Alone, Who has no partner, and we bear witness that Muḥammad is His servant and His messenger, who was sent to creation so that through him they may attain right guidance and certainty. May God bless him, the people of his house and his companions, as long as the sun rises and the lightning sparkles.

1 The author will explain these terms in detail, presenting *ʿibāda*, *ʿubūdiyya* and *ʿubūda* as different forms and levels of worship.

{٢} وبعد، فإنّ درجةَ كمال[١٨] الإنسان برعايةِ وظائفِ خدمةِ[١٩] المعبودِ سبحانه[٢٠]. قال الله تعالى[٢١]: «يا ابنَ آدم! أنا الملك الذي إذا أردتُ أمراً فأقول[٢٢] له[٢٣] كنْ فيكون، وأنا الحيُّ الذي لا يموت، فأطعني أجعلْكَ ملِكاً، إذا أردتَ أمراً[٢٤] فتقول له || كنْ فيكون، وأجعلْكَ حيّاً لا تموت». وقال الله تعالى في محكم تنزيله[٢٥]: ﴿وَمَا خَلَقْتُ الْجِنَّ وَالْإِنْسَ إِلَّا لِيَعْبُدُونِ﴾[٢٦]. [ب ٤٤ظ]

{٣} وكمال[٢٧] حرّيّة الإنسان عن غير الله[٢٨] على قدر كمال عبادته[٢٩] لله تعالى بدناً، وعبوديّته له[٣٠] قلباً، وعُبُودته[٣١] له[٣٢] روحاً. وهذه المنازل الثلاثة تَحْصُلُ بالمُجاهَدات[٣٣] ثمّ المُكابَدات[٣٤] ثمّ المُشاهدات[٣٥]. فمن بَذَلَ نفسَه في خدمة الله تعالى فهو صاحبُ عبادةٍ[٣٦]، ومن بذل قلبَه في خدمة الله تعالى فهو صاحبُ عبوديّةٍ، ومن بذل روحَه في خدمة الله تعالى فهو صاحبُ عبودةٍ[٣٧]. ||

١٨ أ – كمال.
١٩ ب ح: خذمة.
٢٠ ح – سبحانه.
٢١ ح هـ: مطلب قول الله تع انا الملك الذى.
٢٢ ح: نقول.
٢٣ أ ح – له.
٢٤ ح – أمراً.
٢٥ ح – في محكم تنزيله.
٢٦ سورة الذاريات ٥١/٥٦.
٢٧ ح: وكما.
٢٨ ح + تعالى.
٢٩ ح: عبوديّته.
٣٠ ح + تعالى.
٣١ ح: عبوديّته.
٣٢ ح + تعالى.
٣٣ ب هـ: بالجسد.
٣٤ أ: للمكابدات. ب هـ: بالقلب. كابدت الأمر إذا قاسيت شدته. من **الصحاح**.
٣٥ أ: للمشاهدات. ب هـ: بالروح.
٣٦ أ: عبودية.
٣٧ ح + وقال.

{2} Truly, the degree of human perfection is through observing the duties in the service of the Worshipped One, the Sublime.[2] God the Exalted says [in a *ḥadīth qudsī*]: 'O child of Adam, I am the King, whenever I will something I say to it "Be" and it becomes. I am the Living Who never dies. So obey Me, and I will make you a king, whenever you would will something you will say "Be" and it will become. I will make you alive and you will not die'.[3] God the Exalted also says in His clear revelation: 'I created the jinn and humankind only to worship Me' [Q 51:56].

{3} The perfection of one's freedom from anything other than God is commensurate to his worship of God the Exalted with the body (*'ibāda*), his servanthood to Him with the heart (*'ubūdiyya*), and his servitude to Him with the spirit (*'ubūda*).[4] These three stations occur through striving, endurance, and witnessing.[5] He who offers his self (*nafs*) in the service of God the Exalted is called *ṣāḥib 'ibāda*, or man of worship. He who offers his heart (*qalb*) in the service of God the Exalted is called *ṣāḥib 'ubūdiyya*, or man of servanthood. And he who offers his spirit (*rūḥ*) to the service of God the Exalted is called *ṣāḥib 'ubūda*, or man of servitude.

2 The necessary human-Divine relation is clear, according to Samarqandī, there is the *Ma'būd*, and the *'abd*, and so being human correctly is to act in conformity and awareness of this relationship.

3 For a slightly different narration (*riwāya*) of this *ḥadīth qudsī*, see Abū Ḥāmid al-Ghazālī, *al-Mawā'iẓ fī l-aḥādīth al-qudsiyya*, in *Majmū'at rasā'il al-Imām al-Ghazālī*, ed. Ibrāhīm Amīn Muḥammad, Cairo: al-Maktaba al-Tawfīqiyya, (n.d.), pp. 608-23, at p. 613.

4 The more perfect one's service to God the greater his/her freedom. It indicates that human beings obtain their freedom by serving God. Here Samarqandī is telling us that true freedom is to serve God with one's body, heart and spirit, which will liberate one from false masters.

5 In the margins of MS Bursa, it is noted that striving is achieved with the body, endurance with the heart and witnessing with the spirit.

وقال القشيري قدّس الله روحَه[٣٨]: المنزل الأوّل لِمَن له علمُ اليقين، والثاني لمن له عينُ اليقين، والثالث لمن له حقُّ اليقين. [ح ١١٧و]

{٤} ثمّ نقول: تركيب[٣٩] ع-ب-د يقتضي التذلُّلَ في اللغة، يقال للطريق المُذَلَّل بكثرة وَضْعِ الأقدام عليه: الطريقُ[٤٠] المُعَبَّدُ، ويقال للثوب الصَّفِيق: || ثوبٌ ذُو عَبَدَةٍ[٤١]. والأَنَفَةُ والعَبَدَةُ[٤٢] مترادفان لاستلزام الأنفةِ الذُّلَّ، ومنه البِدْعَة إذ فيها الهوانُ والخزيُ، ومنه الدُّعابَة[٤٣] إذ المِزاحُ[٤٤] يُزيل المَهابةَ[٤٥]. ولذلك قال المشايخ رحمهم الله[٤٦]: التواضعُ يُضِيءُ جوهرَ[٤٧] العبوديّةِ والتكبُّرُ يُكَدِّرُه، إذ التواضعُ يُحَقِّقُه والتكبّرُ ينافيه[٤٨]. ومصداقه قول الله تعالى[٤٩]: [ب ٤٥و]

---

٣٨ ح: رحمه الله تعالى.
٣٩ ح + عبد.
٤٠ ح: الطريقة.
٤١ ح – ويقال للثوب الصفيق: ثوب ذو عبدة؛ ب – ثوب ذو عبدة.
٤٢ أ ب: والعبد.
٤٣ ح: الدُباعة.
٤٤ ح: أمر المزاح.
٤٥ ب هـ: الدُّعابَة المِزاحُ وقد دَعَبَ وهو دعّابٌ لعَّابٌ والمُداعَبَةُ الممازحَةُ. من **الصحاح**.
٤٦ ح + تعالى. ح هـ: مطلب في أن التواضع يضيء جور العبودية.
٤٧ ح: جور.
٤٨ ح: إذ التواضع والتكبّر ينافيان.
٤٩ ح هـ: مطلب في قوله تعالى العظمة إزاري والكبرياء ردائي فمن نازعني في شيء منهما ألقيته في النار ولا أبالي.

Qushayrī, may God sanctify his spirit, said[6] that the first station belongs to those who possess the knowledge of certainty (*'ilm al-yaqīn*); the second (station) to those who possess the vision of certainty (*'ayn al-yaqīn*), and the third (station) to those who possess the reality of certainty (*ḥaqq al-yaqīn*).[7]

{4} We further say: Linguistically the root *'-b-d* means lowliness (*tadhallul*). A well-trodden path (*al-ṭarīq al-mudhallal*) is called a beaten path (*al-ṭarīq al-mu'abbad*), and a thick garment is called a garment of strength (*thawb dhū 'abada*). Scorn (*al-anafa*) and disdain (*al-'abada*) are synonymous, for scorn necessitates lowliness; religious innovation (*bid'a*) is part of it, as it involves disgrace and ignominy; also jesting is part of it, for joking eradicates dignity. Therefore scholars, may God show them mercy, have said: Humility (*tawāḍu'*) illuminates the essence of servanthood, while arrogance (*takabbur*) taints it, for humility is in harmony with servanthood, while arrogance opposes it.[8] The confirmation of this is to be found in the statement of God the Exalted:

6 See Abū l-Qāsim 'Abd al-Karīm al-Qushayrī, *al-Risāla al-qushayriyya*, ed. 'Abd al-Ḥalīm Maḥmūd and Maḥmūd ibn al-Sharīf, Cairo: Dār al-Ma'ārif, (n.d.), vol. 2, p. 347; Abu '-l-Qasim al-Qushayri, *Al-Qushayri's Epistle on Sufism*, trans. Alexander D. Knysh, Reading: Garnet Publishing, 2007, p. 210.

7 Here the three degrees of certainty are linked to the well-known threefold categorization of religion: *islām*, *īmān* and *iḥsān*, set out clearly in the Hadith of Jibrīl. When the body submits, the result is called *'ibāda*, traditionally understood to refer to the outward practices of religion. When the body is surrendered, the heart is opened to the light of *īmān*; what Samarqandī calls *'ubūdiyya*. Finally comes *'ubūda*, still from the same Arabic root, which denotes the state of a human being who has reached the highest degree of certainty, which is *ḥaqq al-yaqīn*. And this is considered the real freedom, because someone at this high degree is genuinely indifferent to his or her own needs and preferences, but seeks only conformity with God's nature and commandments. In sufi tradition, often such freedom expresses itself in the form of giving service to others. While many scholars come up with correspondences for these three dimensions of religion (*islām, īmān, iḥsān*), this linking with three different forms of *'-b-d* is done quite beautifully by Samarqandī.

8 Here we see why the worst of the deadly sins is pride, or *kibr*. It is a form of defiant ignorance. God alone has Lordship; because He Alone is *al-Ḥaqq*, the Real. To depend on anyone or anything else is a kind of idolatry, because it suggests that they can offer help in ways that the Almighty cannot or will not. Hence pride is a kind of *shirk* or polytheism which will be further elaborated by Samarqandī in subsequent passages.

«العظمةُ إزاري والكبرياءُ ردائي، فمن نازَعَني فيهما ألقيتُه في النار ولا أُبالي». والإزارُ والرداءُ كنايةٌ[٥٠] عن نفي الشركَة، لأنّ الإزار والرداء لا يكونان مشترَكَيْنِ في المُتَعارَف؛ أو الإزارُ كنايةٌ عن صفات قُدْسِه، والرداءُ كنايةٌ عن صفات جمالِه وكمالِه[٥١].

{٥} **فُرَيْعَة**[٥٢]: العبادة مغايرةٌ للطاعة، إذ العبادةُ عبارةٌ عن كمال التذلُّل فلا يَحِلُّ إلّا[٥٣] لله تعالى، ولذلك قالوا: المعبودُ اسمُ الله تعالى || على الخصوص لا يُطلقُ على غيره، والطاعةُ[٥٤] عبارةٌ عن امتثال الأمرِ، ولذلك سُمِّيَ ضدُّها المعصية وهي تركُ الأمر، وبضدّها تتبيَّنُ الأشياءُ[٥٥]، فيجوز[٥٦] الطاعةُ لغير الله تعالى، قال الله تعالى: ﴿أَطِيعُوا اللَّهَ وَأَطِيعُوا الرَّسُولَ وَأُولِي الْأَمْرِ مِنْكُمْ﴾[٥٧]. || [ب ٤٥ظ]

{٦} **فصل** في أقوال المشايخ الصوفيّة في بيان العبادة والعبوديّة على حسب أحوالهم ومقاماتهم. [ح ١١٧ظ]

{٧} قال ذو النون المصري[٥٨] رحمه[٥٩] الله: "العبوديّة أن تكونَ عبدَه في كلِّ حالٍ كما أنّه[٦٠] ربُّك في كلِّ حالٍ".

---

٥٠ ح: كنايتان.

٥١ ب: وحكي عن بعض أهل المعرفة أنه قال كتمانُ الطاعة مفتاح الإخلاص، وترك الشهوات مفتاح الخلاص، والتقوى مفتاح الجنّة، وحسنُ الخلق مفتاح الوصول إلى الحقيقة.

٥٢ أ: فشريعه؛ ح: دقيقة. ح هـ: مطلب في أن العبادة مغايرةٌ للطاعة.

٥٣ أ – إلّا.

٥٤ ح – عبارة عن كمال التذلّل فلا يَحِلُّ إلّا لله تعالى ولذلك قالوا المعبودُ اسمُ الله تعالى على الخصوص لا يُطلقُ على غيره والطاعة.

٥٥ ح – وبضدّها تتبيّن الأشياء.

٥٦ أ: يجوز.

٥٧ سورة النساء ٥٩/٤.

٥٨ أ – المصري.

٥٩ ب: رحمهم.

٦٠ ح + تعالى.

'Magnificence is My covering and grandeur is My robe. Whoever contends with Me for either of them, I shall cast him into the Fire and will not care!'[9] The 'covering' and the 'robe' may allude to the rejection of partnership, for they cannot be [simultaneously] shared, as it is commonly known. Or the 'covering' may refer to His attributes of holiness, while the 'robe' may stand for His attributes of beauty and perfection.[10]

{5} A short subsection: Worship (*'ibāda*) is different to obedience (*ṭā'a*). For worship means perfection of lowliness and is not permissible to be directed to anyone other than God the Exalted. Therefore, it is said: The name the Worshipped One (*ma'būd*) belongs exclusively to God and cannot be applied to anyone other than Him. Obedience on the other hand stands for following a command, and therefore its opposite is named 'insubordination' (*ma'ṣiya*), meaning disobeying a command, and it is through their opposites that things become clear. It is permissible to obey others than God the Exalted, as God the Exalted says: 'Obey God, and obey the Messenger, and those of you who are in authority' [Q 4:59].[11]

{6} A section on the words of sufi masters regarding worship and servanthood in accordance with their states and stations:

{7} Dhū l-Nūn al-Miṣrī [d. c. 245/859], may God show him mercy, said: 'Servanthood means to be His servant in every condition just as He is your Lord in every condition'.[12]

9 This hadith is reported with a slightly different wording in Abū Dāwūd, *Sunan*, "al-Libās", 28, nr. 4092.

10 In the margins of MS Bursa there is a comment which states: 'It is reported about one of the people of knowledge that he said: "Secrecy in obedience is the key to sincerity, abandonment of carnal desires is the key to deliverance, God-fearfulness is the key to the Garden, and beautiful character is the key to attaining the *ḥaqīqa*"'.

11 Here Samarqandī turns his attention to the consequence of servitude which he understands to be not a passive and receptive state but rather, something needing to be confirmed in how human beings act. The first expression of this sincere surrender comprises the forms of worship which should be dedicated to God alone. Again, this is an obedience which reveals human freedom. To surrender to divine reality is not like any other surrender; it is a liberation.

12 This is about consistency in serving God, which is a sign of interior surrender, indicating that the outward (*ẓāhir*) and the inward (*bāṭin*) are in harmony.

{٨} وقال أبو علي الورّاق[٦١] رحمه الله[٦٢]: "أنتَ عبدُ مَنْ أنت في رقِّه وأَسْرِه[٦٣]. إن كنتَ في أسر[٦٤] نفسِك فأنتَ عبدُ نفسِك، وإن كنتَ || في أسر[٦٥] دنياك فأنتَ عبدُ دنياك، وإن كنتَ في أسر[٦٦] مولاك ورقِّه فأنتَ عبدُ مولاك"[٦٧]. ومصداقُه قول النبي عليه السلام[٦٨]: «تَعِسَ[٦٩] عبدُ الدرهمِ، تَعِسَ عبدُ الخَمِيصَة»[٧٠]. [أ ٩٢و]

{٩} ورأى[٧١] أبو يزيد[٧٢] البسطامي قدّس الله روحَه وكثّر فُتوحَه[٧٣] || رجلًا فقال[٧٤]: "ما حِرْفَتُك؟" فقال الرجل[٧٥]: "خَرْبَنْدَه"، فقال: "أماتَ اللّهُ[٧٦] حمارَك[٧٧] لِتَكونَ عبدَ الله[٧٨] لا عبدَ حمارِك". [ب ٤٦و]

{١٠} قال عبد الله بن مبارك[٧٩] رحمه الله[٨٠]: "العبد عبدٌ ما لم يطلُبْ لنفسِه خادماً، فإذا طَلَبَ لنفسِه خادماً فقد سَقَطَ عن حدِّ العبوديّة".

٦١ أ: الدقاق.
٦٢ ح – رحمه الله.
٦٣ ح + وأمره.
٦٤ ح: أمر.
٦٥ ح: أمر.
٦٦ ح: أمر.
٦٧ أ ب: فانت عبده.
٦٨ ح: صلى الله تعالى عليه وسلم.
٦٩ ح هـ: أي هلك.
٧٠ ب هـ: الخميصة كساءٌ اَسْوَدُ مُرَبَّعٌ له عَلمانِ، فإن لم يكن مُعلماً فليس بخميصة. من **الصحاح**.
٧١ ب: ويَرأى؛ ح: قال.
٧٢ أ ح: زيد.
٧٣ ح: رح.
٧٤ ح – فقال.
٧٥ أ ب – الرجل.
٧٦ ح + تعالى.
٧٧ ح + أمات الله تع حمارك.
٧٨ ح + تع.
٧٩ أ: منازل.
٨٠ ب – رحمه الله؛ ح + تع.

{8} Abū ʿAlī al-Warrāq [d. c. 3rd/9th century], may God show him mercy, said: 'You are the servant of that in whose bondage and captivity you are; if you are in the captivity of your ego, then you are the servant of your ego; if you are in the captivity of your worldly life, then you are the servant of your worldly life; and if you are in the captivity of your master and in his bondage, then you are the servant of your master'.[13] The confirmation of this is to be found in the words of the Prophet, peace be upon him: 'Wretched is the slave of the dirham, wretched is the slave of the *khamīṣa* [i.e. fine garment]'.[14]

{9} Abū Yazīd al-Bisṭāmī [d. 261/874-5 or 234/848-9], may God sanctify his spirit and increase his (spiritual) openings, saw a man and asked him: 'What is your profession?' The man responded: 'ass-herd' (*kharbanda*). He then said: 'May God make your donkey die so that you become a servant of God and not a servant of your donkey!'[15]

{10} ʿAbd Allāh ibn [al-]Mubārak [d. 118/736 or 181/797], may God show him mercy, said: 'The servant is a servant until he seeks a servant for himself; and when he seeks a servant for himself then he falls out of the realm of servanthood'.[16]

13 This is to underline the point made earlier: everyone is an *ʿabd*, we all have our objects, places and people we love and adore. We can love and serve those things for selfish reasons, for some personal gain; or we can love and serve them because we make the basic theological mistake of assuming that they really have power over us. In both cases we are *ʿabd*. But we can also serve the true Master. So, according to this statement which Samarqandī quotes, as well as those that follow, the clear indication is that in every case the human is a slave; the question is only: to whom or to what.

14 See Ibn Mājah, *Sunan*, "al-Zuhd", 8, nr. 4274.

15 There is a play of words here, assuming the dialogue was held in Persian, since ass-herd or *kharbanda* literally means 'servant of donkey', while *khudābanda* indicates 'servant of God'.

16 Here the idea of *ʿubūdiyya* is explained in the context of *zuhd*, i.e. holy poverty and renunciation. One's servanthood to God can be compromised by the heart's connectedness to worldly things.

{١١} وقال أبو حفص الحدّاد رحمه الله: "العبوديّة زينةُ العبد، فمن تَرَكَها تَعَطَّل من الزينة"[٨١].

{١٢} وقال أبو إسحاق الكلاباذي البخاري رحمه الله: "الخواصُّ لم يَترُكُوا وظائفَ العبادة ترْكَ مُعانِدٍ، ولم يعتمِدُوا عليها اعتمادَ معوِّلٍ[٨٢]، بل راعوها حقَّ الرعاية واعتمدوا على ما قُسِم لهم في السابق وكُتب لهم في الذكر"[٨٣].

{١٣} وقال بعضهم: "كمال العبوديّة في عدم السكون والطمأنينة على اللّذّة أو الكرامة وعدم الاعتماد على وظائف البرِّ والتقوى"[٨٤].

{١٤} وقال الواسطي[٨٥]: "احْذرُوا لذّةَ العطاء، فإنّما هي غِطاءٌ لأهل الصفاء. وقال الله تعالى: ﴿وَأَنَّ إِلَى رَبِّكَ الْمُنْتَهَى﴾"[٨٦].

---

٨١ ح – وقال أبو حفص الحدّاد رحمه الله: العبوديّة زينة العبد، فمن تَرَكَها تعطّل من الزينة.

٨٢ ب: مُعَوَّلٍ. ب هـ: كما يقال عَوِّل عليَّ بما شِئْتَ أي اسْتعِن بي كانّه يقول احْمِلْ عليَّ ما احببتَ وما له في القوم من مُعَوَّلٍ والاِسْمُ العَوْلُ. من **الصحاح**.

٨٣ ح – وقال أبو إسحاق الكلاباذي البخاري رحمه الله: الخواصّ لم يتركوا وظائفَ العبادة تركَ معاندٍ ولم يعتمدوا عليها اعتمادَ معوّلٍ، بل راعوها حقَّ الرعاية واعتمدوا عل ما قُسّم لهم في السابق وكُتب لهم في الذكر.

٨٤ ح – وقال بعضهم: كمال العبوديّة في عدم السكون والطمأنينة على اللّذة أو الكرامة وعدم الاعتماد على وظائف البرّ والتقوى.

٨٥ ح + ره.

٨٦ سورة النجم ٤٢/٥٣. ح – وقال الله تعالى: ﴿وَأَنَّ إِلَى رَبِّكَ الْمُنْتَهَى﴾.

{11} Abū Ḥafṣ al-Ḥaddād [d. c. 265/878-9], may God show him mercy, said: 'Servanthood is the adornment of a servant; whoever abandons it becomes hindered from the adornment'.[17]

{12} Abū [Bakr Muḥammad ibn] Isḥāq al-Kalābādhī al-Bukhārī [d. 380/990], may God show him mercy, said: 'The spiritual elite have not abandoned the duties of worship in the manner the obstinate one abandons them. Neither have they relied upon them the way the one with false confidence relies presumptuously on them. Rather, they have truly observed (the duties of worship) and relied upon what had been formerly assigned to them and prescribed for them in the Qur'an'.

{13} Some of them [i.e. sufi masters] said: 'The perfection of worship is in the absence of rest or of reassurance of delight or esteem, and the absence of self-satisfaction in the tasks of piety and God-fearfulness'.[18]

{14} [Abū Bakr] al-Wāsiṭī [d. c. 320/932] said: 'Beware of the delight of gifts, for it is a covering [i.e. barrier][19] for the people of purity. As God the Exalted said: "and that your Lord, He is the goal"' [Q 53:42].

17 This saying uses an aesthetic approach. To serve God sincerely is to be an integrated human being, whose outward obedience is in harmony with his inner state, and thus perceived by others to be beautiful.

18 According to Samarqandī, we should not rely on our good actions and piety, because ultimately it is the divine mercy and kindness that saves us, not our own actions. It is not due to our acts that we deserve heavenly life; everything is a gift from God including our good actions as they are facilitated by Him. This resonates with Samarqandī's words in his *'Aqīda*: 'Complete thankfulness for the outward and inward blessings of God is not possible, because every instance of thanks for a new blessing requires further thanks unendingly. A blessing from God, even if it be small, cannot be praised without incurring new blessings such as power, protection, time, space and so forth. The attainment of Heaven and salvation from punishment are only possible due to His mercy and His favour, not because we deserve them by our deeds. [...] Acts of worship and other good deeds do not necessarily bring about happiness [i.e. salvation] and entry into Heaven. Neither do sinful acts necessarily bring about wretchedness [i.e. damnation] and entry into Hell. Happiness and entering Heaven, as well as wretchedness and entering Hell, are only due to the mercy of God and His justice'. See Demiri, "God and Creation", p. 101.

19 *Ghiṭā'* or covering indicates ignorance of perceiving the truth, as in the Qur'anic verse 50:22: '(And to the evil-doer it is said): You were in heedlessness of this. Now We have removed from you your covering (*ghiṭā'ak*), and piercing is your sight this day'.

{١٥} وقال الجنيد رحمه الله[٨٧]: "العبوديّة تركُ الأشغال، والاشتغالُ[٨٨] || بالشغلِ[٨٩] الذي هو أصلُ الفراغة"[٩٠]. [ب ٤٦ظ]

{١٦} وقالوا[٩١]: "اين كار كسى نيست كه كارى دارد"[٩٢].

{١٧} وقال السيّد أبو القاسم الشهيد السمرقندي رحمه الله: "العبادةُ أن تفعلَ ما يرضاه الربُّ تعالى[٩٣]، والعبوديّةُ أن ترضى بما فعل الربُّ"[٩٤].

{١٨} وقال بعض[٩٥] || المشايخ رحمهم الله: "مجموعُ أمورِ الشريعة والطريقة منحصرٌ في أمرين: [ح ١١٨و]

(١) أن تعمل لله[٩٦] خالصاً عن[٩٧] شوائب الشرك الجليِّ والخفيِّ[٩٨]؛ (٢) وأن تَرْضَى بما قضَى اللهُ تعالى وقدَّر، والله هو المُوَفِّق والمُسَدِّد"[٩٩].

---

٨٧ أ + رحه.
٨٨ ح: والاشغال.
٨٩ أ: فالشغل.
٩٠ ح: الفراعنة.
٩١ ب – وقالوا.
٩٢ ح – وقالوا: اين كار كسى نيست كه كارى دارد.
٩٣ ح – تعالى.
٩٤ ح – تعالى.
٩٥ ح + المشايخ رح.
٩٦ ح + تعالى.
٩٧ ح: من.
٩٨ ب هـ: الشوب الخلط يعني عمله لا يكون مخلوطا بالشرك الجلي وهو الشرك بالله والشرك الخفي هو الرياء.
٩٩ ح: والمرشد.

{15} Al-Junayd [al-Baghdādī, d. 298/911], may God show him mercy, said: 'Servanthood is to abandon occupations, and to be occupied with the occupation which is the essence of release'.[20]

{16} They also said: 'This is not the occupation of someone who has an occupation'.[21]

{17} Al-Sayyid Abū l-Qāsim al-Shahīd al-Samarqandī [d. 556/1161],[22] may God show him mercy, said: 'Worship (*'ibāda*) means to do that which the Lord the Exalted is pleased with, and servanthood (*'ubūdiyya*) means to be pleased with that which the Lord the Exalted does'.[23]

{18} Some of the masters, may God show them mercy, said: 'The totality of issues of *sharī'a* and *ṭarīqa* is confined to two matters:

(1) to act purely for the sake of God, free from any stains of *shirk*,[24] be it clear or hidden, and (2) to be pleased with whatever God the Exalted determined and made happen. And God is the Provider of success and right direction'.[25]

20 In other words, servanthood is to avoid any distractions which would divert you from the true purpose of your creation, which is to worship the Creator. Servanthood is further defined as *the* occupation which will set you free from all worries and concerns. It is to devote oneself exclusively to Him, Who in turn will ease your anxieties and set you free.

21 Here also the message is that servanthood is *the* occupation for which all other occupations should be abandoned. Special thanks to Reza Pourjavady for his help in translating this Persian sentence.

22 Nāsir al-Dīn Muḥammad ibn Yūsuf al-Ḥusaynī, a Ḥanafī jurist, the author of *al-Fiqh al-nāfi'*.

23 Here worship (*'ibāda*) is described in relation to compliance, that the servant's actions should be in complete obedience and harmony with the divine decree and pattern in the world. Whereas servanthood (*'ubūdiyya*) implies the degree of *riḍā*: to be well-pleased with whatever God does in His creation: the bitter and the sweet of His decree, for the person of *'ubūdiyya* knows that His decree is always from His perfect wisdom.

24 Literally *shirk* means 'ascribing a partner to God', or 'worshipping others beside God', and is often translated as polytheism or idolatry.

25 This resonates with the Qur'anic verse: 'God is pleased with them and they are pleased with Him' (Q 9:100 and 98:8). Here *riḍā* is related to sincerity in dealing with God. His servants must act purely for Him in sincerity.

{١٩} **دقيقة**: لكلّ حِرْفَةٍ حانوتٌ وآلاتٌ تَتَأَدَّى بها، فحانوتُ هذه الحِرفَة – أعني العبادة – الخلواتُ، وآلاتُها المَعِدَةُ الخاليةُ[١٠٠].

{٢٠} **تنبيه**: الدعاء مخُّ العبادة وخالصُها بفتوى نبيّنا عليه السلام، ولِما ذكرنا أنّ العبادة والعبوديّة والعبودة عبارةٌ عن التذلُّل، والدعاءُ محضُ التضرُّعِ[١٠١]، وقال الله تعالى[١٠٢]: ﴿ادْعُونِي أَسْتَجِبْ لَكُمْ إِنَّ الَّذِينَ يَسْتَكْبِرُونَ عَنْ عِبَادَتِي سَيَدْخُلُونَ || جَهَنَّمَ دَاخِرِينَ﴾[١٠٣]، أي[١٠٤] عن دعائي، هكذا نقل عن أهل التأويل رحمهم الله[١٠٥]. [ب ٤٧و]

{٢١} وقال الفقهاء نصرهم الله تعالى: العبادةُ على أقسامٍ[١٠٦]:

{١/٢١} عبادةٌ بدنيّةٌ محضةٌ حسنةٌ لِعَيْنِها كالصلاة[١٠٧]، لأنّها بُنِيَت على حركاتٍ وسكناتٍ أُعِدَّتْ لتعظيم الله[١٠٨]، وتعظيمُ الله[١٠٩] حسنٌ ومقصودٌ لذاته.

---

١٠٠ ح – دقيقة: لكلّ حِرْفَة حانوتٌ وآلات تتأدّى بها، فحانوتُ هذه الحِرفَة أعني العبادة الخلوات، وآلاتها المعدةُ الخاليةُ.
١٠١ ح: فصل ولما ذكرنا أن العبادة والعبودية عبارة عن التذلّل والتضرّع لقول النبي صلى الله تعالى عليه وسلم الدعاء مخّ العبادة وخالصها.
١٠٢ أ – تعالى.
١٠٣ سورة غافر ٦٠/٤٠.
١٠٤ أ هـ: أي صاغرين.
١٠٥ ح – رحمهم الله.
١٠٦ ح هـ: مطلب فى أقسام العبادات.
١٠٧ ح: كالصلوات.
١٠٨ ح + تع.
١٠٩ ح + تع.

{19} A subtle point: Every occupation has its workplace and tools through which it is performed. And the workplace of this occupation, namely worship, is the place of seclusion, and its tool is the empty stomach.[26]

{20} A note: Prayer (*duʿāʾ*) is the quintessence of worship and its purest (form), according to the Prophet's instruction.[27] As we mentioned earlier, worship (*ʿibāda*), servanthood (*ʿubūdiyya*) and servitude (*ʿubūda*) consist of lowliness [i.e. humility], and so prayer is sheer self-abasement. And God the Exalted says: 'Pray to Me and I will hear your prayer; those who are too proud to serve Me, they will enter Hell, disgraced' [Q 40:60], that is '(those who are too proud) to pray to Me'. Thus it is transmitted by the exegetes, may God show them mercy.

{21} Jurists, may God the Exalted support them, say: Worship is of different kinds.

{21.1} Purely bodily worship, beautiful in itself, such as *ṣalāt*, for it involves movements and pauses all intended to glorify God, and glorification of God is beautiful and is intended for itself.

26 After the emphasis on the crucial importance of sincerity in worship, here Samarqandī turns his attention to the manner through which this can be facilitated: in a state of seclusion, away from people's eyes, and by avoiding any indulgence in worldly pleasures.

27 Here the author is referring to two sayings of the Prophet: 'Prayer is the quintessence of worship' (*al-duʿāʾ mukhkh al-ʿibāda*) and 'Prayer is worship itself' (*al-duʿāʾ huwa l-ʿibāda*). See Tirmidhī, *Sunan*, "al-Daʿawāt", 2, nr. 3698 and 3699.

{٢/٢١} وبدنيّةٌ محضةٌ حسنةٌ[١١٠] لِغيرها كالصوم، لأنّه شُرِع لِقَهْر النفس الشهويّة وتصفيةِ الباطنِ لله تعالى لِيَسْلَمَ القلبُ والروحُ والبدنُ[١١١] عن شوائب[١١٢] العوائق عن الخدمة، قال الله تعالى لداود عليه السلام: «عادِ نفسَك، فإنّها انْتَصَبَتْ لمُعاداتي»، فيكون الصومُ البغضَ في الله[١١٣]. وأشار إلى ما ذكرنا قولُ الله تعالى: ﴿يَا أَيُّهَا الَّذِينَ آمَنُوا[١١٤] كُتِبَ عَلَيْكُمُ الصِّيَامُ كَمَا كُتِبَ عَلَى الَّذِينَ مِنْ قَبْلِكُمْ لَعَلَّكُمْ تَتَّقُونَ﴾[١١٥].

{٣/٢١} وعبادةٌ ماليّةٌ محضةٌ[١١٦] حسنةٌ لغيرها كالزكاة، لأنّ حُسْنَها || لحاجة الفقير. والحكمة في شرعها: تصفيةُ الباطن[١١٧] || عن رَذِيلة البُخلِ، وشكرُ نعمة المال، والشفقةُ على عباد[١١٨] الله تعالى[١١٩]. [ح ١١٨ظ] [ب ٤٧ظ]

{٤/٢١} وعبادةٌ فيها معنى المَؤُونَة كصدقة الفِطْر والعُشْر، فإنّهما عبادتان من حيثُ || شُكر نعمة المال، ومَؤُونَةٌ[١٢٠] من حيث إنّهما سببان لبقاء المال بدُعاءِ الفقراءِ. والمَؤُونَة مَفْعُلَةٌ[١٢١] من الأيْن وهو التعبُ فيكون المؤونة تحمُّل مشقّةِ الغير شرعاً لطلب منافِعِه، أو فَعُولَةٌ[١٢٢] من المَوْن[١٢٣] وهو الإقاتةُ. [أ ٩٢ظ]

---

١١٠ ح – حسنة.
١١١ ح – والبدن.
١١٢ أ هـ: موانع.
١١٣ ح + تع. ب هـ: أي بغضُ النفس لأنها عدوُّ الله تعالى.
١١٤ أ ب – يَا أَيُّهَا الَّذِينَ آمَنُوا.
١١٥ سورة البقرة ١٨٣/٢.
١١٦ أ ب: محضة مالية.
١١٧ ح: للباطن.
١١٨ ح: عبادة.
١١٩ ب – تعالى.
١٢٠ ح – ومؤونة.
١٢١ أ: فعوله.
١٢٢ أ: مفْعُله؛ ب + مَفْعَلَةٌ.
١٢٣ ح: الموت.

{21.2} Purely bodily worship, beautiful for something other than itself, such as fasting, for it is prescribed in order to subdue the passioned ego and to purify the inward (*bāṭin*) for the sake of God the Exalted so that the heart and the spirit and the body may be free from blemishes that hinder service. God the Exalted said to David, peace be upon him: 'Treat your ego with enmity, for it stands against Me in hostility',[28] and so fasting becomes anger for the sake of God. The following words of God the Exalted indicate what we have just mentioned: 'O you who believe! Fasting is prescribed for you, as it was prescribed to those before you, so that you may ward off (evil)' [Q 2:183].[29]

{21.3} Purely monetary worship, good for something other than itself, such as *zakāt*, for its goodness is due to the need of the poor. And the wisdom behind its being prescribed as a duty is to purify the inward (*bāṭin*) from the vice of stinginess, to be grateful (to God) for the blessing of wealth and to treat servants of God the Exalted with compassion.[30]

{21.4} Worship in the meaning of provision (*ma'ūna*), such as *ṣadaqat al-fiṭr* (alms given upon the completion of Ramadan) and *'ushr* (tithe). These two are acts of worship, since (they involve) gratitude for the blessing of wealth. (There is a sense of) maintenance (*ma'ūna*), due to the fact that these two are the reasons for the continuation of the wealth, thanks to the prayers of the poor. The *ma'ūna* follows the pattern *maf'ula* from the root *ayn* meaning fatigue, and so the *ma'ūna* indicates the bearing of the hardship of the other [as prescribed] by *sharī'a* for their benefit. Or it is the case that the *ma'ūna* follows the pattern *fa'ūla* from the root *mawn* meaning to provide sustenance.

28 This *ḥadīth qudsī* is quoted in 'Alī ibn Muḥammad al-Āmidī, *al-Iḥkām fī uṣūl al-aḥkām*, ed. 'Abd al-Razzāq 'Afīfī, Riyadh: Dār al-Ṣumay'ī li-l-Nashr wa-l-Tawzī', 1424/2003, vol. 1, p. 199.

29 This second category includes forms of servitude which are attitudinal, and do not really consist in bodily actions which might be visually appreciated. Fasting is the key example here: it is invisible. So worship does not denote only an action; it can equally refer to the disciplined absence of an action: in this case, eating, drinking and sexual pleasure.

30 The *zakāt* is worship, an act of surrender to God; it is a sacrifice, an offering. Here the servitude has a moral amplitude: the needy are served for the glory of God.

{٥/٢١} وعبادةٌ بدنيّةٌ وماليّةٌ[١٢٤] حسنةٌ لغيرها كالحجّ، فإنّ حُسْنَه لشرفِ الكعبة، وهو عبادةُ هِجْرَةٍ[١٢٥] في الله[١٢٦] لتعظيمِ بِقاعٍ مُشرَّفةٍ.

{٦/٢١} وعبادة هي فرضُ كفايةٍ كالغزو[١٢٧]، فإنّ حسْنَه لإعلاء[١٢٨] الدين ودفعِ الفتنة، فإذا حَصَل هذا بالبعض سقط عن الباقين، ولا يَبْقَى مشروعاً إذا أَسْلَمَ الكلُّ كما يكون في زمن عيسى عليه السلام بعد نزوله من السماء خليفةً لنبيِّنا عليه السلام[١٢٩]. والله[١٣٠] أعلم بحقائق أحكامه. ||

{٢٢} **دِعامةٌ**: العباداتُ والعبوديّاتُ ومِلاكُهما أمران: إذنُ الشارعِ والإخلاصُ[١٣١]. [ب ٤٨و]
فإنّ عبادات[١٣٢] الراهِبِين[١٣٣] وعبوديّاتهم[١٣٤] مردودةٌ وسببٌ لمزيدِ البُعْد عن الله تعالى[١٣٥] واستحقاقِ الدركاتِ[١٣٦]، لأنّها واقعةٌ لا على قانون الشريعة[١٣٧]. وكذا بِدَعُ المبتدعةِ وعباداتُ المُرائِين مردودةٌ، لأنّ الشرك الخفيَّ والجليَّ[١٣٨] || مُحْبِطان[١٣٩] [ح ١١٩و]
للأعمال. قال الله تعالى:

١٢٤ أ ب: محضة.
١٢٥ ح – هجرة.
١٢٦ ح + تع.
١٢٧ ح: وعبادة بدنية مالية حسنة لغيرها كالغزو وهو فرض كفاية.
١٢٨ ح: كاعداء.
١٢٩ ح – ولا يبقى مشروعاً إذا أسلم الكلّ كما يكون في زمن عيسى عليه السلام بعد نزوله من السماء خليفةً لنبيّنا عليه السلام.
١٣٠ ح + تع.
١٣١ ح: فصل ينبغى أن يكون العبادة والعبودية بأمرين يعني بإذن الشرع والإخلاص.
١٣٢ ح: عبادة.
١٣٣ أ: الرهابين.
١٣٤ ح: وعبوديتهم.
١٣٥ ب – تعالى.
١٣٦ ح – واستحقاق الدركات.
١٣٧ ح: الشرع.
١٣٨ ح: لأن الشرك الجليّ بالله والخفي مبطلان.
١٣٩ ح: مبطلان.

{21.5} Bodily and monetary worship, good for something other than itself, such as *ḥajj*. Its beauty is due to the nobleness of the Kaaba. It is worship consisting of migration to God in order to honour noble sites.

{21.6} Worship that is a collective duty, such as military expeditions. Their goodness is due to elevating the religion, and repelling anarchy (*fitna*). When this is achieved by means of some, then the duty falls from the rest. It will no longer be legitimate when everyone submits, as it will be in the time of Jesus, peace be upon him, after his descent from heaven to serve as the caliph of our Prophet, peace be upon him. God knows best the truths of His precepts.

{22} A pillar [i.e. principle]: There are two essential prerequisites for the acts of worship and servanthood: (1) Permission from the Law-Giver [i.e. God], and (2) Sincerity (*ikhlāṣ*). Surely the acts of worship made by monks and their servanthood are rejected; they increase their distance from God the Exalted and lead them to stages downwards. For they occur not upon the law of *sharīʿa*. So too the innovations of the people of *bidʿa* and the acts of worship performed by the ostentatious are rejected, for *shirk*, be it hidden or open, makes works void.[31] God the Exalted says [in a *ḥadīth qudsī*]:

31 Samarqandī is becoming somewhat legalistic here. He identifies preconditions for the validity of the acts of worship. First, divine permission is necessary, since to approach God is the most important and significant human act; it is the reason for the creation of man and jinn, as he explained earlier. Therefore, it cannot be done in a casual or willful way. Hence the risk of *bidʿa*; one cannot simply use their own preferences and whims to determine the manner of their response to the Real. Nobody can concoct a new form of *ʿibāda*, for a perfect discipline of worship has been gifted in revelation. Second, the text also reminds us that form is no substitute for content. Actively insincere praying, for instance, to impress someone, is equated with *shirk*.

«أنا أغْنَى الشُّرَكاءِ عن الشرْكِ، فمن عَمِلَ[١٤٠] عملًا وأشْرَكَ فيه مَعِيَ غيري تَرَكْتُه وشِرْكَهُ». وقال النبي عليه السلام[١٤١]: «يقال للمُرائِي يومَ القيامة: يا غادِر، ويا خاسِر! الْتَمِسْ أَجرَك ممّن كنتَ تعملُ له!»[١٤٢].

{٢٣} آفة العبادة: [(١) الفترةُ؛ (٢) حبُّ المدح؛ (٣) العُجْبُ]

{١/٢٣} الفترة. قال النبي عليه السلام: «لكلّ شيء آفة، وآفة العبادة الفترة». وقال الشاعر:

لكلٍّ إلى[١٤٣] شَأْوِ الْعُلَى حركاتُ ولكن عزيزٌ في الرجال ثباتُ

وقال المشايخ رحمهم الله: الفترة في الطريقة حرامٌ على أهل الطريقة، وهي[١٤٤] الإعراض عن التصوّف والإقبالُ إلى الغفلات والدنيا، وهي ارتدادٌ في الطريقة[١٤٥].

---

١٤٠ أ ب + لي.

١٤١ ح: صلى الله تعالى عليه وسلم. ح هـ: مطلب يقال يوم القيمة للمرائى يا غادر ويا خاسر التمس أجرك ممّن كنت تعمل له.

١٤٢ ح + فصل الوقفة مباحة فى بعض الأوقات، وهى التلذّذ بالنعم المباحة والاستراحة للتقوى على الوظايف، قال أمير المؤمنين علي كرّم الله تعالى وجهه لا تكرهوا القلوبَ واطلبوا نشاطها فإنها إذا أكرهت عميت، وقال نبيّنا صلى الله تعالى عليه وسلم لا تشدّدوا على أنفسكم فيشدّد الله تعالى عليكم فانّ قوما شدّدوا على أنفسهم شدّد الله تعالى عليهم.

١٤٣ أ – إلى.

١٤٤ ب: وهو.

١٤٥ ح: فصل قال النبي صلى الله تعالى عليه وسلّم لكل شيء آفة وآفة العبادة ثلثة. أحدها الفترة وهى الإعراض عن التصوّف والإقبال إلى غفلات الدنيا، وقال المشايخ رحمه الله تعالى الفترة في الطريقة حرام على أهل الطريقة وارتداد فيها.

'I am the One Who is most free from want of partners. Whoever performs a deed in which he associates another besides Me, I will abandon him with his *shirk*'.[32] The Prophet, peace be upon him, says: 'On the day of resurrection the ostentatious will be told: "O deceitful, O loser, ask your reward from that which you worked for"'.[33]

{23} Calamities of worship[34] [are three: languor, love of praise and conceit].

{23.1} [The first calamity of worship is] languor (*fatra*). The Prophet, peace be upon him, said: 'Everything has a calamity and the calamity of worship is languor'.[35] The poet said:

> 'Everyone requires movements to [reach] the peak of heights;
> yet valued is stability by men'.[36]

And the masters, may God show them mercy, said: 'Languor in the path (*al-ṭarīqa*) is impermissible to the people of the path; for it means turning away from *taṣawwuf* and drawing near to heedlessness and the world, and this is relapse (*irtidād*) in the path.[37]

32 Muslim, *Ṣaḥīḥ*, "al-Zuhd wa-l-raqā'iq", 6, nr. 7666.

33 This is part of a longer narration which is, for instance, found in Abū 'Abd Allāh al-Qurṭubī, *al-Jāmiʿ li-aḥkām al-Qur'ān*, ed. 'Abd Allāh ibn 'Abd al-Muḥsin al-Turkī, Beirut: Mu'assasat al-Risāla, 1427/2006, vol. 1, pp. 35-6.

34 In other words, calamities which may compromise worship. What is meant by calamity here is *āfa*, which might also be translated as defect or drawback. The message Samarqandī gives is that every positive human act is beset by potential pitfalls; even worship, and one will do well to study and take precautions against these stumbling blocks.

35 The hadith is recorded in Abū l-Qāsim Sulaymān ibn Aḥmad al-Ṭabarānī, *al-Muʿjam al-kabīr*, ed. Ḥamdī 'Abd al-Majīd al-Salafī, Cairo: Maktabat Ibn Taymiyya, (n.d.), vol. 3, pp. 66-8, nr. 2688.

36 These verses are attributed to Abū l-Qāsim 'Abd al-Wāḥid ibn Muḥammad ibn 'Alī ibn al-Ḥarīsh al-Iṣbahānī (d. 424/1033). See Abū Manṣūr 'Abd al-Malik al-Thaʿālibī, *Yatīmat al-dahr fī maḥāsin ahl al-ʿaṣr*, ed. Mufīd Muḥammad Qamīḥa, Beirut: Dār al-Kutub al-ʿIlmiyya, 1403/1983, vol. 5, p. 136.

37 It is noteworthy that Samarqandī has chosen the word *irtidād* here, which is normally used to indicate apostasy. This comparison shows that for the people of the path, standards are high. Languor or slackness would eventually lead to abandonment of the path.

[ب ٤٨ظ] والله تعالى مثَّل[١٤٦] بَلْعَمَ بن[١٤٧] باعُوراء[١٤٨] بالكلبِ || اللاهِث، لإعراضه عن الطريقة وإقبالِه || على الدنيا في قوله تعالى: ﴿وَلَوْ شِئْنَا لَرَفَعْنَاهُ بِهَا وَلَٰكِنَّهُ أَخْلَدَ إِلَى الْأَرْضِ وَاتَّبَعَ هَوَاهُ فَمَثَلُهُ كَمَثَلِ الْكَلْبِ إِنْ تَحْمِلْ عَلَيْهِ يَلْهَثْ أَوْ تَتْرُكْهُ يَلْهَثْ﴾[١٤٩]. [ح ١١٩ظ]
وقال بعض مشايخنا رحمهم الله: "گرد ما مگرد چون گشتی برمگرد"[١٥٠]. الوقْفةُ مباحةٌ في بعض الأوقات[١٥١]، وهي التلذُّذُ بالنِّعَم المباحة والاستراحةُ لِلتَّقَوِّي على الوظائف. قال أمير المؤمنين عليّ رضي الله عنه وكرَّم وجهَه[١٥٢]: "لا تُكْرِهُوا القلوبَ واطلبُوا نشاطَها، فإنّها إذا أُكْرِهَتْ عَمِيَتْ". قال نبيّنا عليه السلام[١٥٣]: «لا تُشَدِّدُوا على أنفسكم فيُشَدِّدَ اللهُ[١٥٤] عليكم، فإنّ[١٥٥] قوماً شَدَّدُوا على أنفسهم فشَدَّدَ[١٥٦] اللهُ[١٥٧] عليهم، فتلك بَقاياهُم في الصوامِع والدِّيارات، ﴿رَهْبَانِيَّةً ابْتَدَعُوهَا مَا كَتَبَ اللَّهُ عَلَيْهِمْ﴾»[١٥٨].

---

١٤٦ ح: شبّه.
١٤٧ أ – بن.
١٤٨ ب: بَاعُور.
١٤٩ سورة الأعراف ١٧٦/٧.
ب هـ: اللُّهاثُ بالضمّ حَرُّ العطش، ولهَثَ الكَلْبُ بالفتح يَلْهَثُ لَهْثاً ولُهاثا بالضمّ إذا أخرجَ لسانه من التعب أو العَطَش، وكذلك الرجُل إذا اعْيا، وقوله تعالى إن تحمِلْ عليه يَلْهَثْ لأنك إذا حملتَ على الكلب نبَحَ وَوَلَّى هاربا وإن تركتَهُ شَدَّ عليك ونبح فيُتعِبُ نفسَه مُقبلاً عليك فيَعْتَرِيه عند ذلك ما يَعْتَريه عند العطش من اخراج اللّسان. من **الصحاح**.
١٥٠ ح – وقال بعض مشايخنا رحمهم الله: گرد ما مگرد چون گشتی برمگرد.
١٥١ ح هـ: مطلب في أن التلذذ مباحة في بعض الأوقات لنشاط قلبه إلى العبادة والطاعة.
١٥٢ ح: علي كرّم الله وجهه.
١٥٣ ح: صلى الله تعالى عليه وسلّم.
١٥٤ ح + تعالى.
١٥٥ أ: وإن.
١٥٦ ح: شدد.
١٥٧ ح + تعالى.
١٥٨ سورة الحديد ٢٧/٥٧: ﴿وَرَهْبَانِيَّةً ابْتَدَعُوهَا مَا كَتَبْنَاهَا عَلَيْهِمْ إِلَّا ابْتِغَاءَ رِضْوَانِ اللَّهِ فَمَا رَعَوْهَا حَقَّ رِعَايَتِهَا﴾.

God the Exalted likened Bal'am son of Bā'ūrā' to a panting dog with his tongue out, due to his turning away from the path and drawing near to the world, in the following words of the Exalted: 'And had We willed, We could have raised him by their means, but he clung to the earth, and followed his own lust. Therefore, his likeness is as the likeness of a dog: if you drive him away he pants with his tongue out, and if you leave him alone he still pants with his tongue out' [Q 7:176]. Some of our masters, may God show them mercy, said: 'Do not come close to us;[38] if you [happen to] come close, do not go away'.[39] However, taking a pause from time to time is permissible, which means tasting the permissible blessings and resting to regain strength for further duties. The commander of the believers, 'Alī [ibn Abī Ṭālib], may God be pleased with him and ennoble his face, said: 'Do not coerce your hearts, instead seek their vivacity, for when they are coerced, they become blind'. Similarly, our Prophet, peace be upon him, said: 'Do not be hard on yourselves lest God treats you hardly; a group of people were hard on themselves and so God treated them hardly; those are their remainders in the hermitages and monasteries; "monasticism they invented, God ordained it not for them" [Q 57:27]'.[40]

38 Literally: do not circle us.

39 The emphasis is on the need and importance of continuity in servanthood and worship. Special thanks to Reza Pourjavady for his help in translating this Persian sentence.

40 See Qur'anic verse: '[...] But monasticism they invented – We ordained it not for them – only seeking God's pleasure, and they observed it not with right observance [...]' (Q 57:27). The hadith is reported in Abū Dāwūd, *Sunan*, "al-Adab", 52, nr. 4906.

وقال شهاب الدين السهروردي قدّس الله روحه: || "أشبع الزنجي وكُدَّهُ"[١٥٩]. [ب ٤٩و]

{٢/٢٣} والآفة الثانية: حُبُّ المدْحِ. فإنّ العبادة لحبِّ مدحِ الخلقِ وتعظيمِهم في المجالِس نوعُ[١٦٠] شرْكٍ. قال أهل التفسير: جاء رجل إلى نبيّنا عليه الصلاة والسلام[١٦١] فقال: يا رسول الله[١٦٢] إنّي أُراعِي العباداتِ لكنّي أُحِبُّ مدحَ الناس بي[١٦٣] لأجلها، فنزَلَ قولُه تعالى: ﴿فَمَنْ كَانَ يَرْجُو لِقَاءَ رَبِّهِ فَلْيَعْمَلْ عَمَلاً صَالِحًا وَلَا يُشْرِكْ بِعِبَادَةِ رَبِّهِ أَحَدًا﴾[١٦٤].

{٣/٢٣} والآفة الثالثة: العُجْبُ[١٦٥]، فإنّه يَخْدِشُ وجوهَ العبادات. وفي حديث معاذٍ رضي الله[١٦٦] عنه قال النبي صلّى الله تعالى عليه وسلّم[١٦٧]: «إنّ لله تعالى ملائكةً في بعض || أبواب السماوات يَرُدُّون[١٦٨] أعمالَ المُعْجَبِين». والله[١٦٩] العاصمُ عن كلِّ آفةٍ. [أ ٩٣و]

١٥٩ ح – الوقفة مباحةٌ في بعض الأوقات، وهي التلذّذ بالنعم المباحة والاستراحة للتقوى على الوظائف. قال أمير المؤمنين عليّ رضي الله عنه وكرّم وجهه: لا تُكْرِهُوا القلوبَ واطلبوا نشاطَها، فإنّها إذا أُكْرِهَتْ عَمِيَتْ. قال نبيّنا عليه السلام: لا تُشَدِّدُوا على أنفسكم فيشدّد الله عليكم، وإنّ قوماً شدّدوا على أنفسهم فشدّد الله عليهم، فتلك بقاياهم في الصوامع والديارات رهبانية ابتدعوها ما كتب الله عليهم. وقال شهاب الدين السهروردي قدّس الله روحه: أشبع الزنجي وكُدَّهُ.

١٦٠ ح + من.

١٦١ أ – عليه الصلاة والسلام؛ ح: النبي صلى الله تعالى عليه وسلّم.

١٦٢ ح + تع.

١٦٣ أ ب – بي.

١٦٤ سورة الكهف ١٨/١١٠.

١٦٥ ح + فى بعض أبواب السموات يرد عمل العجب.

١٦٦ ح + تع.

١٦٧ أ ب – قال النبي صلّى الله تعالى عليه وسلّم.

١٦٨ أ ب: يردّ.

١٦٩ ح + تع.

Shihāb al-Dīn al-Suhrawardī [d. 587/1191], may God sanctify his spirit, said: 'Gratify the slave and you will make him work hard'.[41]

{23.2} The second calamity [of worship] is love of praise (*ḥubb al-madḥ*). To worship God because of love for people's praise and their regard in gatherings is a kind of *shirk*.[42] (Qur'an) commentators say that a man once came to our Prophet, peace and blessings be upon him, and said: 'O Messenger of God, I observe acts of worship, but I also like it when people praise me for those acts'. Upon this the following words of God the Exalted were sent down [Q 18:110]: 'And whoever hopes for the meeting with his Lord, let him do righteous work, and make none sharer of the worship due to his Lord'.[43]

{23.3} The third calamity [of worship] is conceit (*'ujb*). It causes scratch marks on the face of the acts of worship.[44] According to a hadith, narrated by Mu'ādh, may God be pleased with him, the Prophet, may God the Exalted bless him and grant him peace, said: 'God the Exalted has angels in front of some of the doors of heavens; they turn back the deeds of the conceited'.[45] However, God alone is the deliverer from every calamity.[46]

41 The allusion being that your body needs food in order to be able to carry on with worship. This saying is, however, attributed to Sufyān al-Thawrī (d. 161/778) in the *Iḥyā'*. See Abū Ḥāmid al-Ghazālī, *Iḥyā' 'ulūm al-dīn*, Beirut: Dār al-Ma'rifa, 1982, vol. 3, p. 95.

42 In other words, this is *al-shirk al-khafī*, the hidden polytheism or idolatry, which was earlier mentioned by Samarqandī a number of times.

43 See, for instance, Abū Ja'far Muḥammad ibn Jarīr al-Ṭabarī, *Jāmi' al-bayān 'an ta'wīl āy al-Qur'ān*, ed. 'Abd Allāh ibn 'Abd al-Muḥsin al-Turkī, Cairo: Hijr li-l-Ṭibā'a wa-l-Nashr wa-l-Tawzī' wa-l-I'lān, 1422/2001, vol. 15, pp. 440-1.

44 Here Samarqandī emphasizes the lethal risk of feeling pleased with oneself. This makes a nonsense of the prayer, because the prayer, as Samarqandī observes, is the outward and inward enactment of *tadhallul*, of self-abasement in the glorious presence of the Real. In Samarqandī's view, a prayer which ends in self-praise is likely to find rejection in the balance of heaven.

45 I have not been able to locate any hadith sources that include this narration.

46 In the end, Samarqandī reminds the reader not to lose hope, for God has the power to deliver us from all kinds of calamity, including the calamities of prayer. It is a theology of hope that he recommends, a complete reliance in God, trust in His mercy and kindness.

{٢٤} **قانونٌ كلّيٌّ**: الاستقامةُ[١٧٠] في جميع الأعمال والأخلاق واجبةٌ، وهي الاحترازُ عن طرفي الإفراط والتفريط. قال النبي عليه السلام: «دينُ اللّٰه بين الغلوِّ والتقصيرِ». فالميلُ إلى تصفية الروحِ وإهمالِ القالبِ إهمالًا || كلّيّاً عادةُ [ب ٤٩ظ] المُتَقَشِّفَةِ[١٧١] والرهابين. والميلُ إلى تصفيةِ القالبِ والإعراضِ عن تصفية الرُّوحِ وتَحْلِيَتِها عادةُ المُتْرَفِين وأهلِ الصورةِ من المُتَعبِّدِين. وكلاهما مذمومٌ[١٧٢]، لأنّ[١٧٣] الإنسان[١٧٤] مركّبٌ من الروحِ والقالبِ، وإنّهما شريكان في الإكرام والإهانةِ. وأمْرُ ﴿فَاسْتَقِمْ كَمَا أُمِرْتَ وَمَنْ تَابَ مَعَكَ﴾[١٧٥] عامٌّ في جميع الخصالِ المَلَكيّة والسَّبُعِيّة والبهيميّة، والاستقامةُ مِن أصْعَبِ المقامات، ولذا قال النبي صلّى اللّٰه عليه وسلّم[١٧٦]: «شيّبَتْني سورة هود»[١٧٧]. واللّٰه الميسِّر لكلِّ عسيرٍ[١٧٨].

---

١٧٠ ب هـ: قال السري الاستقامة أن لا يختار على اللّٰه شيئاً، وقال عالم الاستقامة الخوف من عزيز الجبّار والحبّ النبي المختار والحياء من الملايكة الحُضار، عن عبد اللّٰه بن مسعود عن أبيّ أنه قال والذى نفس محمّد بيده لا يستقيم إيمان عبد حتّى يستقيم لسانه ولا يستقيم لسانه حتّى يستقيم قلبه، وحكي عن بعض أهل الرياضة أنه قال استقامة اللسان على الذكر والثناء، واستقامة النفس على الطاعة والحياء، واستقامة القلب على الخوف والرجاء، واستقامة الروح على الصدق والصفاء، واستقامة السرّ على اليقظة والوفاء، من أخلص الخلصاء.

١٧١ ب هـ: المتقشّفة المتزهّدة الدين يحرمون على أنفسهم الطيّبات وهم عبّاد الكذّاب، وقيل المتقشّفة الذي يتبلّغُ بالمَقُوت وبالمرقّعِ. من **الصحاح**.

١٧٢ أ: مذمومان.

١٧٣ أ – لأنّ.

١٧٤ أ: فالإنسان.

١٧٥ سورة هود ١١/١١٢.

١٧٦ أ: عليه السلام.

١٧٧ أ ب ح + عليه السلام.

١٧٨ ح – قانونٌ كلّيٌّ: الاستقامة في جميع الأعمال والأخلاق واجبةٌ وهي الاحتراز عن طرفي الإفراط والتفري. قال النبي عليه السلام: دين اللّٰه بين الغلوّ والتقصير. والميلُ إلى تصفية الروح وإهمالِ القالبِ إهمالاً كلّيّاً عادةُ المُقَشِّفَةِ والرهابين، والميلُ إلى تصفية القالب والإعراضِ عن تصفية الروح وتحليتِها عادةُ المُتْرَفين وأهلِ الصورةِ من المُتَعبّدين، وكلاهما مذمومان. فالإنسان مركّبٌ من الروح والقالبِ، وإنّهما شريكان في الإكرام والإهانةِ. وأمر فاستقم كما أمرت ومن تاب معك عامٌّ في جميع الخصال المَلَكيّة والسَّبُعيّة والبهيميّة، والاستقامةُ من أصعب المقامات، ولذا قال النبي عليه السلام: شيّبَتْني سورة هود عليه السلام. واللّٰه الميسِّر لكلِّ عسيرٍ.

{24} A general principle: Integrity (*istiqāma*) is necessary in all deeds and morals, and this means guarding against the two extremities of excessiveness (*ifrāṭ*) and deficiency (*tafrīṭ*). The Prophet, peace be upon him, says: 'The religion of God is between excessiveness and deficiency'.[47] Inclination towards purification of the spirit, while completely neglecting the outward form [i.e. body] is the custom of rough ascetics and monks. And inclination towards refinement of the outward form, while avoiding the purification of the spirit and its embellishment is the custom of indulgent people and the only superficially pious. Both of these are reprehensible, for a human being is composed of a spirit and a body, and they both have a share in ennobling (one) or degrading. The [Qur'anic] instruction [in the verse 11:112]: 'So keep to the right course as you have been commanded, together with those who have turned to God with you' is an all-inclusive command, referring to all traits, be they angelic or bestial. Integrity [or being upright, following the middle way], is the most difficult of stages (*maqāmāt*). Therefore, the Prophet, may God bless him and grant him peace, said: 'Sūra Hūd has made me age'.[48] And God is the Giver of ease for all difficulties.[49]

47 Abū Muḥammad 'Uthmān ibn 'Abd Allāh ibn al-Ḥasan al-'Irāqī al-Ḥanafī, *al-Firaq al-muftariqa bayna ahl al-zaygh wa-l-zandaqa*, ed. Yaşar Kutluay, Ankara: Nur Matbaası, 1961, p. 8.

48 The hadith is reported as *shayyabatnī Hūd* (Hūd has made me age) in Tirmidhī, *Sunan*, "Tafsīr al-Qur'ān", 56, nr. 3609.

49 Here *istiqāma* is described as balance: rectitude as finding and maintaining due balance between excess and inadequacy. It is noteworthy that Samarqandī ends on this note of balance and wisdom. His message is clear: as well as the balance between inward and outward, there is the balance between body, mind and spirit, and the balance between doing too much and doing too little.

{٢٥} **الشرط المهمّ**[١٧٩] لأهل الخلوات والأربعينات إحضارُ القلب لذكر الله تعالى، لأنّ الذهْنَ متى توَجَّه إلى أمرٍ أعْرَضَ عن الباقي، فإذا شُغِل القلبُ[١٨٠] بذكر الله تعالى[١٨١] وهو المقصودُ الأعظمُ[١٨٢] || خلا عن الباقي لا محالة. فمن [ح ١٢٠و] خلَّى قلبَه عن الذكر[١٨٣] وأرسلَه || في أودية الوساوس[١٨٤] أو الهَواجِسِ[١٨٥] في [ب ٥٠و] الخلوات[١٨٦] يكون ذا عُزلةٍ عن أهل الإسلام مُخالطاً مُصاحباً لكافرٍ وهو الشيطان أو عدوٍّ من[١٨٧] أعداء الله تعالى وهو النفس، وإنّه خارجٌ عن الشريعة والطريقة. والله المرشد والمسدِّد[١٨٨].

{٢٦} والحمد لله ربّ العالمين وصلوات الله وسلامه على خير خلقه محمّد وآله وصحبه وعلى جميع إخوانه من الأنبياء والمرسلين. تمّت رسالة العبوديّة بحمد الله ومنِّه[١٨٩].

---

١٧٩ ح: اعلم أنّ الشرط المهمّ.
١٨٠ أ: أشغل قلبَه؛ ب: شغل قلبَه.
١٨١ ب – تعالى.
١٨٢ ح + خلا.
١٨٣ أ ب – عن الذكر.
١٨٤ ب ح: الوسواس.
١٨٥ ح: أو الهواء.
١٨٦ ح – في الخلوات.
١٨٧ ح: ومن.
١٨٨ ح: والله المسدد والمرشد.
١٨٩ أ + تمت علم الدقايق بعون الله تعالى وحسن توفيقه؛ ح + تمت رسالة العبودية بحمد الله تعالى ومنّه، والصلوة والسلام على سيّدنا محمد عليه السلام وآله وصحبه أجمعين، والحمد لله ربّ العالمين.

{25} The important precondition for the people of seclusions and forty-day retreats is to prepare the heart for remembering God the Exalted, because when the mind turns to a certain matter then it diverts from the rest. So, when the heart is occupied with the remembrance of God the Exalted, which is the greatest goal, it surely becomes free from the rest. And so whoever empties his heart of remembrance and releases it to the valleys of devilish insinuations and misgivings, he isolates himself from the people of Islam, associating with and accompanying an unbeliever which is the devil, and one of the enemies of God the Exalted, which is the ego. Thus he departs from the *sharīʿa* and the *ṭarīqa*. God is the Provider of guidance and right direction.

{26} And praised be God the Lord of the worlds, and may His blessings and peace be upon the best of His creation, Muḥammad, his family and companions, and upon all his brethren, the prophets and the messengers. The Treatise on Servanthood is completed with the praise of God and His grace.

Risālat al-Tawba
'Treatise on Repentance'

The present edition is based on the three existing manuscripts of 'Ubayd Allāh al-Samarqandī's *Risālat al-Tawba*, 'Treatise on Repentance':

أ MS Istanbul, Süleymaniye – Ayasofya 2354, fols. 7a-12b (undated).

ح MS Istanbul, Süleymaniye – Hacı Beşir Ağa 387, fols. 132b-138a (undated).

ق MS Kastamonu, Yazma Eser Kütüphanesi – KHK875/03, fols. 50a-51b. (undated) – incomplete, the last third of the text is missing which is replaced by parts of another text including a discussion on the heart (*qalb*), the need for its purification, traits that are perilous and how to get rid of them (fols. 51b-52a).

MS Ayasofya looks older and more accurate than MS Hacı Beşir Ağa which contains some mistakes (misreadings) and gaps (some sentences or passages missing). Though incomplete MS Kastamonu seems to be the most solid and reliable manuscript of the three. It also includes some useful comments in the margins.

Abbreviations:

و	Folio recto
ظ	Folio verso
هـ	Margins of a given manuscript
–	Word/s absent in the manuscript
+	Additional word/s present in the manuscript
[ ]	Word/s added to the text by the editor

رسالة التوبة

Treatise on Repentance

[أ ٧و || ح ١٣٢ظ || ق ٥٠و]

بسم الله الرحمن الرحيم[١]

{١} الحمد لله المفتّحُ[٢] بابُ توبتِه[٣] للمذنبين[٤]، الكريمِ الذي يُنادي كلَّ ليلةٍ رسولُ[٥] حضرته في الملأِ المقرَّبين: «هلْ مِن تائبٍ فَأَتُوبَ عليه»[٦] إظهاراً لكرمه على المحتاجين. وقال في مُحكَم تنزيله: ﴿إِنَّ اللَّهَ يُحِبُّ التَّوَّابِينَ وَيُحِبُّ الْمُتَطَهِّرِينَ﴾[٧]. وشرائفُ[٨] صلواتِه ومدادُ[٩] كلماتِه على من أُرْسِلَ لدعوة أهل الزلّات بالمعجزات النيّرات إلى[١٠] جناب ربّ العالمين محمّدٍ[١١] زُبْدَةِ الكائنات وخلاصةِ الممكنات وعلى آله وأصحابه[١٢] مؤيّدي[١٣] الدين إلى يوم الدين.

١ أ + هذه رسالة التوبة من تأليف الشيخ العالم العامل الزاهد البارع الورع العلّامة ركن الملّة والدين محي السنّة قامع البدعة كاشف مشكلات الشريعة والطريقة عبيد الله بن محمّد السمرقندي قدّس الله روحه ونوّر ضريحه بحقّ محمّد وآله وصحبه.
ق + هذه رسالة التوبة من تأليف الشيخ الإمام العالم العامل الزاهد البارع الورع العلّامة ركن الملّة والدين عزيز الإسلام والمسلمين محي السنّة قامع البدعة كاشف مشكلات الشريعة والطريقة عبيد الله بن محمّد السمرقندي أدام الله علينا ونعمته وبركته وعلى جميع المسلمين. الرسالة في التوبة.

٢ أ ح: مفتّح.

٣ ح: التوبة.

٤ ويمكن قراءتها: الحمد للهِ المفتّحِ بابَ توبتِه.

٥ ق هـ: أراد جبرائيل.

٦ أ: اليه.

٧ سورة البقرة ٢/٢٢٢.

٨ ح: وشريف.

٩ أ: مداد.

١٠ أ – إلى.

١١ ح + صلى الله تعالى عليه وسلم.

١٢ ح + اجمعين.

١٣ ق: مؤيّد.

In the name of God, the Most Merciful, the Compassionate

{1} Praised be God, Whose door of forgiveness is wide open to sinners,[1] the Generous Whose messenger in the heavenly host of the (angels) drawn near, calls every night: 'Is there anyone who repents, that I may accept his repentance?',[2] manifesting His generosity to those in need. As He says in His clear revelation: 'Truly God loves those who turn to Him in repentance and loves those who purify themselves' [Q 2:222].[3] May the noblest of His blessings and the abundance of His words be upon the one sent with luminous miracles to call the people of lapses to the refuge of the Lord of the worlds, Muḥammad the quintessence of existing things and epitome of contingent beings, and upon his family and his companions, the supporters of religion until the Day of Judgement.

1 One may also translate it as: Praised be God, the Opener of the door of His forgiveness to sinners.

2 This is reported in a *ḥadīth qudsī*; Aḥmad ibn Ḥanbal, *Musnad*, ed. Shuʿayb al-Arnaʾūṭ et al., Beirut: Muʾassasat al-Risāla, 1993-2001, vol. 15, p. 362, nr. 9591.

3 *Tawba*, from the verb *tāba-yatūbu* in Arabic, means to turn away from sin and disobedience (with the preposition *ʿan* or *min*) and to return to God (with the preposition *ilā*).

{٢} وبعد، فأيُّها السالكُ ‖ في[١] الطريقة الطالبُ لانفتاح أبواب الحقيقة، إنّ أساسَ السلوكِ التوبةُ النصوحُ. إذ مقامُ التوبة مبدأ المقامات ومفتاحُ[٢] السعادات، فعليك بإحْكامها أوّلاً. فإنّ ثِقلَ الذنوب يمنع النشاط في السير إلى الله تعالى، ونُحُوسَتُها تُورِث الحرمانَ، إذ الإصرارُ على الذنوب يُسوِّدُ القلبَ[٣]، والقلبُ هو السالكُ السائرُ[٤] إلى الله تعالى في الحقيقة. [ق ٥٠ظ]

{٣} وقال النبي عليه السلام[٥]: «إذا أذنبَ ‖ العبدُ نُكِتَ في قلبه نكتةٌ سوداءُ، فإن تابَ صُقِل قلبُه، وإن زاد ازداد[٦] السوادُ إلى أن ران على قلبه»، ثمّ قرأ[٧] قولَ الله عزّ وجلّ[٨]: ﴿كَلَّا بَلْ رَانَ عَلَى قُلُوبِهِمْ مَا كَانُوا يَكْسِبُونَ﴾[٩]، وقال[١٠]: «أيُّها الناسُ توبوا إلى الله[١١]، فإنّي أتوب إليه كلّ يومٍ مائة مرّةٍ»، وقال[١٢]: «إنّه[١٣] لَيُغانُ[١٤] على قلبي، وإنّي[١٥] لأَسْتَغْفِرُ اللهَ تعالى في كلّ يومٍ سبعين مرّةً». [أ ٧ظ ‖ ح ١٣٣و]

١ ح + علم.
٢ ح: مفتح.
٣ ح: القلوب.
٤ ح: والساير.
٥ أ: صلى الله عليه وآله وسلم؛ ح: صلى الله تعالى عليه وسلم.
٦ ح: زاد.
٧ ح + النبى صلى الله تعالى عليه وسلم.
٨ ح: قوله تعالى؛ ق: قول الله تعالى.
٩ سورة المطفّفين ١٤/٨٣.
١٠ أ: قال؛ ح: وقال النبى عليه الصلوة والسلام. ق هـ: أي النبي.
١١ ح + تعالى.
١٢ ح + عليه السلام.
١٣ أ ق: وانه.
١٤ ق هـ: أي يغشى.
١٥ ح: فانّى.

{2} O traveller on the path (to God), seeker of the opening of the doors of *ḥaqīqa*![4] The very foundation of spiritual wayfaring is a sincere repentance.[5] Since the station of repentance is the basis of all stations and the key to all happiness, it is a duty upon you to perform it thoroughly first. Truly, the burden of sins hinders the vigour of journeying to God the Exalted, and its calamitous nature brings deprivation, for persisting in sin blackens the heart, when in reality, it is the heart which travels and journeys to God the Exalted.

{3} The Prophet, peace be upon him, said: 'When a servant commits a sin a black speck is struck on his heart. If he repents his heart is polished, but if he increases [his sinfulness] the blackness increases until it covers his heart with rust'. Then he recited the words of God the Almighty: 'Nay, but that which they have earned is rust upon their hearts' [Q 83:14].[6] (The Prophet) also said: 'O people, turn to God in repentance. Truly, I turn to Him in repentance a hundred times a day'.[7] He further said: 'Sometimes there is a veil over my heart, and I seek forgiveness from God the Exalted seventy times a day'.[8]

4 Indicating special knowledge of the Real, *al-Ḥaqq*, which is a gift directly granted by Him.

5 Samarqandī points out that one enters *ṭarīqa* through *tawba*; the first thing one does in the spiritual journey to God is to repent.

6 See Tirmidhī, *Sunan*, "Tafsīr al-Qur'ān", 74, nr. 3654; Ibn Mājah, *Sunan*, "al-Zuhd", 29, nr. 4385; Abū Muḥammad al-Ḥusayn al-Baghawī, *Maṣābīḥ al-Sunna*, ed. Yūsuf 'Abd al-Raḥmān al-Mar'ashlī et al., Beirut: Dār al-Ma'rifa, 1407/1987, vol. 2, p. 170, nr. 1680.

7 See Muslim, *Ṣaḥīḥ*, "al-Dhikr wa-l-du'ā' wa-l-tawba wa-l-istighfār", 12, nr. 7034; Baghawī, *Maṣābīḥ*, vol. 2, p. 164, nr. 1664.

8 According to another report, 'one hundred times a day'. See Muslim, *Ṣaḥīḥ*, "al-Dhikr wa-l-du'ā' wa-l-tawba wa-l-istighfār", 12, nr. 7033; Abū Dāwūd, *Sunan*, "al-Witr", 26/362, nr. 1517; Baghawī, *Maṣābīḥ*, vol. 2, p. 164, nr. 1663.

{٤} وقال الشيخ شهاب الدين السُّهروردي رحمه الله[١٦]: "المريد[١٧] لا يصل إلى مقام الحقيقة حتّى يُنزِّه نفسَه عن الذنوب عشرين سنةً، وإن وُجِدَتْ منه هَفْوَةٌ[١٨] فيُبادِرُ إلى[١٩] التوبة قبل أن يُصْعَد بها إلى السماء".

{٥} **مسئلة**[٢٠]: التوبة عن[٢١] بعض المعاصي دون البعض صحيحةٌ عند أهل السنّة[٢٢] خلافاً للمعتزلة[٢٣] لقول الله[٢٤] تعالى: ﴿فَمَنْ يَعْمَلْ مِثْقَالَ ذَرَّةٍ خَيْرًا يَرَهُ﴾[٢٥] الآية، وقوله: ﴿وَآخَرُونَ اعْتَرَفُوا بِذُنُوبِهِمْ خَلَطُوا عَمَلًا صَالِحًا وَآخَرَ سَيِّئًا [عَسَى اللّٰهُ أَنْ يَتُوبَ عَلَيْهِمْ إِنَّ اللّٰهَ غَفُورٌ رَحِيمٌ]﴾[٢٦]، وقوله[٢٧]: ﴿وَالْوَزْنُ يَوْمَئِذٍ الْحَقُّ [فَمَنْ ثَقُلَتْ مَوَازِينُهُ فَأُولَئِكَ هُمُ الْمُفْلِحُونَ]﴾[٢٨].

١٦ ح + تعالى؛ ق: السهراوردى رحمة الله عليه. ح هـ: مطلب في قول الشيخ شهب الدين السهروردي لا يصل المريد إلى مقام الحقيقة حتى ينزه نفسه عشرين سنة عن الذنوب.

١٧ ق هـ: أي الذي يطلب طريق الحق.

١٨ ق هـ: الهفوة الذلة وقد هفى هفوة. الهفوة الذلة من غير قصد.

١٩ أ + الى.

٢٠ ح: فصل. ح هـ: مطلب وعند المعتزلة لا تقبل توبة ولا عمل صالح إلّا بترك جميع المعاصي والتوبة عن الكلّ وخطأ هذا لا يخفى.

٢١ ح: من.

٢٢ أ + نصرهم الله؛ ق + نصرهم الله تعالى.

٢٣ يقول عبيد الله السمرقندي في كتابه **العقيدة الركنيّة في شرح لا إله إلّا الله محمّد رسول الله** (تحقيق: مصطفى سنان أوغلي، إستانبول: مركز البحوث الإسلامية، ٢٠٠٨/١٤٢٩، ص ١٢٧): "التوبة عن ذنبٍ واحد صحيحةٌ وإن ارتكب مائةَ كبيرةٍ، وأصرَّ عليها سوى التي تاب عنها، خلافاً للقدرية لإطلاق النصوص". ويقول فيه أيضاً (ص ١٢٨): "التوبة عن الكبائر لا تكون سبباً لمغفرة الصغائر لا محالة عند أهل السنة، خلافاً للمعتزلة؛ ويجوز أنْ يُعَذِّبَ الله تعالى بصغيرة، ويجوز أنْ يعفُوَ عن الكبائر دون الكفر لإطلاق قول الله تعالى: ﴿يُعَذِّبُ مَنْ يَشَاءُ وَيَرْحَمُ مَنْ يَشَاءُ﴾ [سورة العنكبوت ٢١/٢٩]، وقوله: ﴿وَيَغْفِرُ مَا دُونَ ذَلِكَ لِمَنْ يَشَاءُ﴾ [سورة النساء ٤٨/٤]".

٢٤ ح: لقوله.

٢٥ سورة الزلزلة ٧/٩٩.

٢٦ سورة التوبة ١٠٢/٩. ح – الآية، وقوله: ﴿وَآخَرُونَ اعْتَرَفُوا بِذُنُوبِهِمْ خَلَطُوا عَمَلًا صَالِحًا وَآخَرَ سَيِّئًا﴾.

٢٧ ح + تعالى.

٢٨ سورة الأعراف ٨/٧.

{4} Shaykh Shihāb al-Dīn al-Suhrawardī [d. 587/1191], may God show him mercy, said: 'The seeker will not reach the station of *ḥaqīqa* until he distances his soul from sins (*dhunūb*) for twenty years. And if a slip (*hafwa*)[9] occurs in him, he will rush to repentance before it is made to ascend to heaven'.[10]

{5} An issue: To repent for some sinful acts without repenting for some others is valid, according to the Ahl al-Sunna, in opposition to the Muʿtazila,[11] due to the words of God the Exalted: 'And whoever does an atom's weight of good will see it' [Q 99:7], His statement: 'And (there are) others who have acknowledged their sins. They have mixed a righteous action with another that was bad. [It may be that God will accept their repentance. Surely God is Most-Forgiving and Merciful]' [Q 9:102], and His words: 'The weighing (of deeds) on that day is the true (weighing). [As for those whose scale is heavy, they are the successful]' [Q 7:8].

9 As indicated in a sidenote of the manuscript (MS Kastamonu), *hafwa* is equivalent to *dhalla*, meaning to slip, or make a mistake.

10 That is before his soul tastes death.

11 Also in his *ʿAqīda*, Samarqandī gives space to *tawba*, which is unusual for a creedal text. There he says that repentance for one single error is valid, even if one were to commit a hundred grave sins and persist in them. He further notes that unlike the Muʿtazila, according to the Ahl al-Sunna repenting for grave sins (*kabāʾir*) is absolutely not a condition for repenting for lesser sins (*ṣaghāʾir*). God may punish for a lesser sin (*ṣaghīra*), while He may forgive a grave sin (*kabīra*) except for unbelief. For He says: 'He punishes whom He will and shows mercy to whom He will' (Q 29:21) and 'God forgives not that a partner should be ascribed to Him. He forgives (all) save that to whom He will' (Q 4:48). See Samarqandī, *al-ʿAqīda al-rukniyya*, pp. 127-8.

ولو صحّ قولُ المعتزلة يلزم أن لا[٢٩] يوجد وزنُ الأعمال، لأنّ عندهم لا تقبل توبةٌ ولا عملٌ صالحٌ إلّا بترك جميع المعاصي والتوبة عن الكلّ، وخطأ هذا لا يَخْفَى[٣٠].

{٦} **فصل في أقسام التوبة**[٣١]: (١) توبة العوامِّ عن الذنوب الظاهرة؛ (٢) وتوبة الخواصِّ عن الأخلاق الذميمة الباطنة؛ (٣) وتوبة أهلِ البداية من أصحاب الحقيقة وأرباب الكشف عن مواقِعِ || الريبة والشبهة، لأنّ الوقوف في الشبهات سادٌّ لِباب الحقيقة[٣٢]؛ (٤) وتوبة المُحِبِّين عن || الغفلة عن ذكر الله تعالى؛ (٥) وتوبة أهل الكمال من أرباب الحقيقة عن الوقوف على[٣٣] مقامٍ يُتصوَّر أن يكون له وراءَهُ مقامٌ آخر. وعلى هذا[٣٤] أوَّلَ بعضُ المشايخ[٣٥] قولَ النبي عليه السلام[٣٦]: «وإنّي أتوبُ[٣٧] إلى الله تعالى كلّ يومٍ مائة مرّةٍ»، لأنّ النبي عليه السلام[٣٨] كان[٣٩] يترقّى كلَّ يومٍ مائةَ مقامٍ، وإذا وصل[٤٠] إلى مقامٍ استغفرَ عن وُقوفِه فيما سبق[٤١].

[ح ١٣٣ظ]

[أ ٨و]

---

٢٩ اثبتت "أنْ" مفصولةً عن "لا" التزاماً برسم المخطوط، فلعلّ المؤلّف من أتباع أبي حيّان في قوله بالفصل بينهما مطلقاً.

٣٠ ق هـ: أي خطأ قول المعتزلة فيما قالوا.

٣١ ح هـ: مطلب في أقسام التوبة توبة العوام وتوبة الخواص وتوبة أهل البداية من أصحاب الحقيقة.

٣٢ ح هـ: مطلب في أن الوقوف في الشبهات سادّ لباب الحقيقة.

٣٣ ح: إلى.

٣٤ ح + القول.

٣٥ ح + رحمهم الله.

٣٦ أ: عليه الصلوة والسلام.

٣٧ أ ق: لأتوب.

٣٨ أ: صلى الله عليه واله وسلم.

٣٩ ح – كان.

٤٠ ق: وكان إذا وصل.

٤١ ح هـ: مطلب في أن النبي عليه السلام يترقى كل يوم مائة مقام في توجيه قوله إني لأستغفر الله تعالى كل يوم مائة مرة.

Had the opinion of the Mu'tazilites been sound, there would have been no need for the weighing of deeds, for according to them, a repentance or a righteous action is accepted only when all sinful acts are avoided and repentance for all (sins) has taken place. The error of this (opinion) is not hidden.[12]

{6} A section on (different) types of repentance: (1) Repentance of common people from visible sins. (2) Repentance of the elite from hidden blameworthy qualities. (3) Repentance of novices among the people of *ḥaqīqa* and *kashf* from occasions of falling into suspicion and doubt, for persisting in doubts obstructs the door of *ḥaqīqa*. (4) Repentance of lovers (of God) from neglecting the remembrance of God the Exalted. (5) Repentance of the people of perfection among those who have achieved *ḥaqīqa* from pausing at a station when there is another station beyond it.[13] And this is how some of the sufi masters have interpreted the statement of the Prophet, peace be upon him: 'Truly, I turn to God the Exalted in repentance a hundred times a day',[14] for the Prophet, peace be upon him, used to advance a hundred stations every day, and whenever he reached a station he would seek forgiveness for having paused in what preceded.

12 Here Samarqandī seems to be referring to the Mu'tazilī notion regarding grave sins (*kabā'ir*) that God will forgive when the sinner repents. But if there is no repentance there is no divine forgiveness. When it comes to lesser sins (*ṣaghā'ir*), however, God forgives what He wishes to, regardless of whether the sinner repents or not. See, for instance, Qāḍī 'Abd al-Jabbār's (d. 415/1025) views expressed in *Kitāb al-Uṣūl al-khamsa* translated in Richard C. Martin and Mark R. Woodward with Dwi S. Atmaja, *Defenders of Reason in Islam. Mu'tazilism from Medieval School to Modern Symbol*, Oxford: Oneworld, 2003, pp. 90-115, at p. 105.

13 These five types of repentance correspond to five degrees of human perfection. The nearer one is to God the stricter their definition of what constitutes a wrong act necessitating repentance. This is best expressed in the famous saying in Arabic, sometimes attributed to the Prophet, as Samarqandī does in the present treatise: 'The virtues of the pious are the faults of those drawn near to God' (*Ḥasanāt al-abrār sayyi'āt al-muqarrabīn*). See § 21, fn. 50.

14 See Muslim, *Ṣaḥīḥ*, "al-Dhikr wa-l-du'ā' wa-l-tawba wa-l-istighfār", 12, nr. 7034; Baghawī, *Maṣābīḥ*, vol. 2, p. 164, nr. 1664.

وسأل فقيرٌ[٤٢] ملائكةَ اليمين[٤٣] عن توبة أهل الحقيقة، فأجاب بعضُهم بأنّ[٤٤] توبتهم الجلوس في بساط الشهود وإفراد القلب للفرد الحقيقي[٤٥] جلَّ جلالُهُ[٤٦].

{٧} **فصل**: ماهيّة التوبة[٤٧] مُركَّبة من ثلاثة أجزاء: (١) التحسُّرُ والتندّم على ما سبَق، (٢) والانقلاعُ في الحال، (٣) والعزمُ على الامتناع في الاستقبال، هكذا قال فخر الدين الرازي رحمه الله[٤٨] في بعض مصنّفاته[٤٩]. وأمّا إرضاءُ الخصُوم وقضاءُ الفوائت والتصفيةُ عن كدورات المعاصي السابقة، فمِن أوصاف كمالها الخارجةِ عن ماهيَّتها، وإن كانت واجبةً[٥٠].

{٨} ويؤيّدُ ما ذكرنا قولُ الله تعالى: ﴿ثُمَّ يَتُوبُونَ مِنْ قَرِيبٍ فَأُولَئِكَ يَتُوبُ اللّٰهُ عَلَيْهِمْ﴾[٥١]. والقرب: ما وُجد قبل الوفاة ولو بساعةٍ، هكذا فسّره المحقّقون من أهل التأويل والتفسير.

---

٤٢ أ ق + عن.

٤٣ ق: اليمنى.

٤٤ ق: فانّ.

٤٥ ق هـ: أي بحضور القلب تعالى.

٤٦ ح – وسأل فقيرٌ عن ملائكة اليمنى عن توبة أهل الحقيقة، فأجاب بعضُهم بأنّ توبتهم الجلوس في بساط الشهود وإفراد القلب للفرد الحقيقي جلَّ جلالُهُ.

٤٧ ق + أي عين ذاته.

٤٨ ق: رحمة الله عليه.

٤٩ ح – هكذا قال فخر الدين الرازي رحمه الله في بعض مصنّفاته.

٥٠ يقول عبيد الله السمرقندي في كتابه **العقيدة الركنيّة** (ص ١٢٧): "شرط التوبة الندم، والامتناع، والعزم على أن لا يعودَ؛ وليس من شرائط التوبة الثبات عليها إلى الموت، بل التوبة مقبولة بما ذكرنا من الشروط، ولو كان يعودُ إلى المعصية التي تاب عنها في كل يوم سبعين مرّةً لإطلاق النصوص الواردة في التوبة. وأمّا قضاء الفوائت، وأداء الكفّارات الواجبة، وإرضاء الخصوم فذلك شرط لكمال التوبة لا لتحقيق ماهية التوبة. يؤيدُه حكاية الإسرائيلي الذي قتل مائة نفسٍ ثمّ مات بين القريتين على ما عُرفَ في المصابيح وغيره".

٥١ أ: أتوب عليهم. ﴿إِنَّمَا التَّوْبَةُ عَلَى اللّٰهِ لِلَّذِينَ يَعْمَلُونَ السُّوءَ بِجَهَالَةٍ ثُمَّ يَتُوبُونَ مِنْ قَرِيبٍ فَأُولَئِكَ يَتُوبُ اللّٰهُ عَلَيْهِمْ وَكَانَ اللّٰهُ عَلِيمًا حَكِيمًا﴾ (سورة النساء ١٧/٤).

A dervish asked the angels on the right side regarding the repentance of the people of *ḥaqīqa*, and one of them responded that their repentance is to sit on the carpet of witnessing (God) and to devote the heart to the Real One, the Almighty alone.

{7} A section: The very essence of repentance consists of three parts: (1) To grieve and regret what has passed. (2) To desist in the present. (3) Determination to refrain (from it) in the future.[15] This is what Fakhr al-Dīn al-Rāzī [d. 606/1210], may God show him mercy, says in some of his works.[16] As for making amends to one wronged,[17] making up what has passed,[18] and purification from the filth of past transgressions, these are characteristics of its completion that go beyond its essence, although they are required.[19]

{8} What we have mentioned (here) is supported by the words of God the Exalted: 'Then they turn quickly in repentance (to God). These are they toward whom God relents' [Q 4:17].[20] The quickness [mentioned in the verse] indicates (repentance) which takes place before death, even if it be a moment earlier. This is the way the verifiers (*muḥaqqiqūn*) from among the commentators and exegetes have interpreted it.

15 In his *'Aqīda*, Samarqandī further states that the three components mentioned here constitute the preconditions for repentance, namely to regret, to refrain, and to be determined not to go back to the sinful act. See Samarqandī, *al-'Aqīda al-rukniyya*, p. 127.

16 See Fakhr al-Dīn al-Rāzī, *Ma'ālim uṣūl al-dīn*, ed. Ṭāhā 'Abd al-Ra'ūf Sa'd, Beirut: Dār al-Kitāb al-'Arabī, 1404/1984, p. 136.

17 Seeking and obtaining forgiveness of those whom one has wronged.

18 Making up a duty (e.g. prayer) that has been neglected.

19 These are necessary as they enable repentance to be complete, but technically they are not considered part of its very essence.

20 The complete verse: 'God only undertakes to accept repentance from those who do evil in ignorance and then turn quickly in repentance (to God). These are they toward whom God relents. God is All-Knower, Wise' (Q 4:17).

والتوبة[٥٢] من بعيد: ما يوجد بعد الوفاة، قال[٥٣] الله تعالى: ﴿[وَقَالُوا آمَنَّا بِهِ] وَأَنَّى لَهُمُ التَّنَاوُشُ[٥٤] مِنْ مَكَانٍ بَعِيدٍ﴾[٥٥]، وقال النبي صلّى الله تعالى عليه وسلّم[٥٦]: «تُقبل توبةُ العبدِ[٥٧] إذا تاب قبل أن يُغَرْغِرَ»، والغرغَرَةُ تردُّدُ[٥٨] الروح في الحلقِ. || [أ ٨ظ]

{٩} وروي[٥٩] «أنّ واحداً || في[٦٠] الأمم السالفة[٦١] قَتَلَ تسعةً وتسعين[٦٢] نفساً بغير حقٍّ، فأتى راهباً فسأله أنّه: هل تُقبل[٦٣] توبتي إذا تبتُ؟ فقال الراهب: لا، فقتله[٦٤]، ثمّ أتى راهباً آخَرَ فسأله، فقال: لا أعلم ذلك[٦٥]، ولكن في قريب من هذا الموضع قريتان، قريةٌ ليس فيها[٦٦] إلّا أهلُ التقوى يقال لها نَصْرةُ، وقريةٌ ليس فيها[٦٧] إلاّ أهلُ المعصية يقال لها كَفْرةُ، فاقصد إلى نصرة، وأقمْ فيها لعلَّ الله تعالى أن[٦٨] يرحمَك ويتوبَ عليك ببركة أهلها. [ح ١٣٤و]

٥٢ أ ح: فالتوبة.

٥٣ ح: قول.

٥٤ ق هـ: التناؤش بالهمزة التأخّر والتباعد وبغير الهمزة التناول وقوله تعالى وَأَنَّى لَهُمُ التَّنَاوُشُ مِنْ مَكَانٍ بَعِيدٍ يقول أنّى لهم تناول الإيمان في الآخرة وقد كفروا به في الدنيا. من **الصحاح**.

٥٥ سورة السبأ ٥٢/٣٤.

٥٦ أ: صلى الله عليه واله وسلم؛ ح: عليه الصلوة والسلام.

٥٧ ح: البعيد.

٥٨ ح: تردّ.

٥٩ ح هـ: مطلب في توبة من قتل تسعة وتسعين نفساً بغير حقّ وفي نزاع ملائكة الرحمة وملائكة العذاب في قبض روحه فقبض ملائكة الرحمة في آخره لميله إلى أهل الصلاح وأهل التقوى.

٦٠ ح: من.

٦١ ح: السابقة.

٦٢ ق: وتسعون.

٦٣ ق: يقبل.

٦٤ ح: فقتل الراهب.

٦٥ ق – ذلك.

٦٦ أ ق: فيها ليس.

٦٧ أ ق: فيها ليس.

٦٨ ق – أن.

Whereas the delayed repentance means [the regret] that takes place after death, as described in the words of God the Exalted: '[And they will say, "Now we believe in it"], but how can they reach (faith) from such a distant place!' [Q 34:52]. Also the Prophet, may God the Exalted bless him and grant him peace, said: 'The repentance of a servant is accepted when he repents before the death-rattle',[21] and the rattle means the soul moving to and fro in the throat [at the very moment of his death].

{9} It is narrated that a man in one of the earlier communities had killed ninety-nine souls unlawfully, after which he went to a monk and asked him, 'Will my repentance be accepted if I repent?' The monk said, 'No', and he killed (the monk). Then he went to another monk and asked him, and he said: 'I do not know that; however near to this place there are two towns. A town in which there are only Godfearing people, called Naṣra. And a town in which there are only disobedient people, called Kafra. Go to Naṣra and settle there, God the Exalted may show mercy to you, and accept your repentance for the sake of the *baraka* of its people'.

21 See Tirmidhī, *Sunan*, "al-Daʿawāt", 104, nr. 3880; Ibn Mājah, *Sunan*, "al-Zuhd", 30, nr. 4394; Baghawī, *Maṣābīḥ*, vol. 2, p. 171, nr. 1681.

فعمد إليها، فلمّا بلغ الرجلُ[٦٩] إلى موضعٍ هو مَنْصَف بين القريتين دنا[٧٠] وفاتُه، فمال إلى نحو نَصْرةَ ميلاً قليلاً ثمّ مات. فتنازع إليه ملائكةُ الرحمة وملائكةُ العذاب في قبض روحه، فقال الله تعالى: قِيسُوا واذْرَعُوا المسافةَ، فإن وجدتموه[٧١] أقربَ من قرية أهل التقوى بقليل فألحقوه بهم[٧٢]، فقاسُوا فوجدوه أقربَ من قرية أهل التقوى بقليل فألحقوه بأهلها[٧٣]، وقَبِلَ اللّهُ تعالى[٧٤] توبتَه ورَحمَه». ولا شكَّ أنّ أمرَ هذه الأمّة[٧٥] أخفُّ، والربُّ عليهم أَرْأفُ.

{١٠} وقال الشيخ أبو عبد الله محمّد بن خفيف[٧٦] الشيرازي رحمه الله[٧٧]: "توبة أهل الإرادة[٧٨] حلُّ العقود من المَآثِم والاستغفارُ || من اللَّمَم"[٧٩]. [ق ٥١و]

{١١} وأمّا شواهدُ التوبة[٨٠] فردُّ المظالم وإصلاحُ ما فرّط من الفرائض، || ولا يُستَرابُ[٨١] أنّ شاهدَ الشيءِ لا يكون داخلاً في ماهيَّته[٨٢]. [ح ١٣٤ظ]

{١٢} **فصل**: إذا وُجِدَت منك ماهيّةُ التوبة على ما ذكرنا ثمّ نقضتَها فيجب عليك أن تَعُودَ إليها مبادراً، وقُلْ لنفسك: لعلّي أموتُ قبل أن أعودَ إلى الذنب.

---

٦٩ ح – الرجل.
٧٠ ح: دنى.
٧١ ح: وجدت موت.
٧٢ ح: فالحقوا بهم.
٧٣ ح: بهم؛ أ – فقاسوا فوجدوه أقرب من قرية أهل التقوى بقليل فألحقوه بأهلها.
٧٤ ق – تعالى.
٧٥ ح – الأمّة.
٧٦ ح – محمّد بن خفيف.
٧٧ ح – رحمه الله؛ ق: رحمة الله عليه.
٧٨ ق هـ: أي المريد المبتدئ.
٧٩ ق هـ: أي الصغيرة.
٨٠ ح + على ما ذكرنا.
٨١ ق هـ: يعني لا يربط قلبه أنها من الآثام ولكن يحله كله.
٨٢ ح – ولا يُستَرابُ أنّ شاهد الشيء لا يكون داخلًا في ماهيّته.

And so, he made for it. When the man reached a place which is halfway between the two towns, his death drew near. He inclined towards Naṣra for a little bit and then he died. Then angels of mercy and angels of punishment disputed with one another as to who would take his soul, upon which God the Exalted said: 'Measure and calculate the distance. If you find him to be a little nearer to the town of the Godfearing people then add him to them'. So, they measured and found him to be a little nearer to the town of Godfearing people, and they added him to them. And God the Exalted accepted his repentance and showed him mercy.[22] There is no doubt that the matter of this *umma* is less burdened, and that the Lord is more Compassionate towards them.[23]

{10} Shaykh Abū 'Abd Allāh Muḥammad ibn Khafīf al-Shīrāzī [d. 371/982], may God show him mercy, said: 'The repentance of the seekers (of the path)[24] consists of untying knots of sins and seeking forgiveness for offenses'.[25]

{11} As for evidence for repentance, these involve making amends for wrongs[26] and restoration of neglected duties. There is no doubt that evidence of a thing cannot form part of its very essence.

{12} A section: When you accomplish the essential parts of repentance, in accordance with what we have mentioned, and then you violate it, it is incumbent upon you to return to it in haste and say to yourself, 'perhaps I will die before I return to the sinful act'.

22 This hadith appears in multiple reports in Bukhārī, *Ṣaḥīḥ*, "Aḥādīth al-anbiyā'", 57, nr. 3508; Muslim, *Ṣaḥīḥ*, "al-Tawba", 8, nr. 7184-86; Baghawī, *Maṣābīḥ*, vol. 2, pp. 165-6, nr. 1666.

23 Here the emphasis is on the importance of divine mercy which is unlimited. The message is clear: He forgives those who turn to Him in repentance, including those who have committed the gravest of sins.

24 These are novices in the path, according to a note in the margins of MS Kastamonu.

25 Lesser sins, according to a note in the margins of MS Kastamonu.

26 This could be in the form of requiting things or rights that were taken from someone wrongfully and a compensation of any iniquity or acts of injustice.

ولا يَمْنَعَنَّك[٨٣] الشيطان عن التوبة طوراً || ثانياً وثالثاً ورابعاً[٨٤]، هَلُمَّ جرّاً[٨٥]، بأن يقول لك: لا فائدة في توبتك، لا تحفظها! فإنّ ذلك أمارة السعادة لقول النبي عليه السلام[٨٦]: «خيارُكم كلّ مُفتَّنٍ[٨٧] تَوّابٍ»، وقول الله تعالى[٨٨]: ﴿إِنَّ اللَّهَ يُحِبُّ التَّوَّابِينَ﴾[٨٩]. والتوّاب على زِنَةِ الفعَّال للمبالغة، ولا يطلق إلّا على من يُكثِرُ التوبةَ. [أ ٩و]

{١٣} وقال بعض المشايخ رحمهم الله[٩٠]: "كما اتّخذتَ الذنبَ والعودَ إليه حِرفةً، اتّخذِ التوبةَ والعودَ إليها حِرفةً، فلا تكنْ[٩١] في التوبة أعجزَ منك في الذنب. ولو مُتَّ مع ذنبٍ واحدٍ مع التوبة عن سواه من الذنوب السالفة[٩٢]، كان الخوفُ عليك أسهلَ من الموت على الإصرار على الذنوب الكثيرة، فبهذا يُدفَع كيدُ الشيطان". وقال النبي عليه السلام[٩٣]: «ما أَصَرَّ امرؤٌ ولو عاد في اليوم سبعين مرّةً». وسأل واحدٌ[٩٤] عليّاً[٩٥] رضي الله عنه عن هذا، فقال: "عُدْ إلى التوبة كما وقعتَ في الذنب"، قال: "إلى متى؟" فقال: "إلى أن يتحسَّر[٩٦] الشيطانُ ويَعْنَى". واللهِ الموفّق[٩٧].

---

٨٣ ح: يمنعك.
٨٤ ق هـ: أي مرّة بعد مرّة.
٨٥ ق هـ: على هذا إلى ما ورائها في العد.
٨٦ أ: عليه الصلوة والسلام ؛ ح: صلى الله تعالى عليه وسلّم. ح هـ: مطلب في قوله عليه السلام خياركم كل توابٍ.
٨٧ ح – مُفتَّنٍ.
٨٨ ق + عزّ وجلّ.
٨٩ سورة البقرة ٢/٢٢٢.
٩٠ ح + تعالى.
٩١ ق: يكن.
٩٢ ح: الذنوب السابقة أي السالفة.
٩٣ أ: عليه الصلوة والسلام.
٩٤ أ ق + عن.
٩٥ أ ق: عليٍّ.
٩٦ ق هـ: أي تحزّن.
٩٧ أ – والله والموفّق؛ ح – وسأل واحدٌ عن عليٍّ رضي الله عنه عن هذا، فقال: عُدْ إلى التوبة كما وقعتَ في الذنب، قال: إلى متى؟ فقال: إلى أن يتحسَّر الشيطانُ ويعنى. والله الموفّق.

Let not Satan deter you from repentance the second time, the third, the fourth, and so forth, by telling you, 'There is no use to your repentance when you cannot keep it'. In fact it is an indication of (eternal) felicity, as the Prophet, peace be upon him, says, 'The best of you is every tempted one who repents',[27] and God the Exalted says, 'Truly God loves those who turn to Him in repentance' [Q 2:222]. The (form) *tawwāb* follows the pattern of *fa''āl* indicating intensity, and it applies only to those who frequently repent.

{13} One of the shaykhs, may God show mercy to them, said: 'As you have adopted sin and return to it as an occupation, you must adopt repentance and return to it as an occupation. You must not be more incompetent in repenting than you are in sinning. There would be less concern about you if you were to die with one sin while you had repented for all your other earlier sins, rather than to die while persisting in numerous sins. Thus Satan's ruse can be repelled'. The Prophet, peace be upon him, said: 'One should not persist [in the sinful act], even if he were to return [to it] seventy times a day'.[28] Someone asked 'Alī [ibn Abū Ṭālib], may God be pleased with him, about this, and he said: 'Return to repentance just as you have fallen into the sin'. He further asked: 'Until when?' And he [i.e. 'Alī] responded: 'Until Satan is weary and distressed'. God is the One Who grants Success.[29]

27 This hadith is recorded in al-Bazzār's *Musnad*: Abū Bakr Aḥmad al-Bazzār, *al-Baḥr al-zakhkhār*, ed. Maḥfūẓ al-Raḥmān Zayn Allāh, Beirut: Mu'assasat 'Ulūm al-Qur'ān, 1409/1988, vol. 2, p. 280, nr. 700.

28 According to a report recorded in Abū Dāwūd, *Sunan*, "al-Witr", 26/362, nr. 1516; Tirmidhī, *Sunan*, "al-Da'awāt", 121, nr. 3907; Baghawī, *Maṣābīḥ*, vol. 2, p. 170, nr. 1678: 'He who has asked for forgiveness should not persist [on the sinful act], even if he were to return [to it] seventy times a day' (*mā aṣarra man istaghfara wa-in 'āda fī l-yawmi sab'īna marratan*).

29 In his *'Aqīda*, Samarqandī further notes that persisting in repentance (i.e. refraining from the sinful act) until death is not one of the preconditions of repentance. Repentance is accepted when properly done, even if one were to return seventy times a day to the sinful act of which one had repented before. See Samarqandī, *al-'Aqīda al-rukniyya*, p. 127.

{١٤} **فصل في الفرق بين التوبة والأَوْبَة والإنابة**[٩٨]: قال الإمام البُشاغري[٩٩] في عصمة الأنبياء عليهم السلام[١٠٠]: "التوبة الرجوع عن الذنب، والأَوْبةُ الرجوع عن[١٠١] الخير إلى رؤية التوفيق والنعم، والإنابة الرجوع[١٠٢] عمّا سوى الله تعالى"[١٠٣]. قال الله تعالى[١٠٤]: ﴿يَا أَيُّهَا || الَّذِين آمَنُوا تُوبُوا إِلَى اللهِ تَوْبَةً نَصُوحًا عَسَى رَبُّكُمْ أَنْ يُكَفِّرَ عَنْكُمْ سَيِّئَاتِكُمْ﴾[١٠٥]، وقال في وصف أيّوب عليه السلام[١٠٦]: ﴿نِعْمَ الْعَبْدُ إِنَّهُ أَوَّابٌ﴾[١٠٧]، مَدَحَه[١٠٨] اللّٰهُ || تعالى بالتسليم ورؤيةِ البلاء والنعم، فصَبَر وشكرَ لله تعالى[١٠٩] في حال البلاء والنعمة، وقال: ﴿مَنْ خَشِيَ الرَّحْمٰنَ بِالْغَيْبِ وَجَاءَ بِقَلْبٍ مُنِيبٍ﴾[١١٠]. [ح ١٣٥و] [أ ٩ظ]

٩٨ ح هـ: مطلب في التوبة بين التوبة والأوبة والإنابة.
٩٩ ح + رحمه الله.
١٠٠ ح – في عصمة الأنبياء عليهم السلام.
١٠١ أ: الى.
١٠٢ ح + إلى الله تعالى.
١٠٣ ق + عزّ وجلّ.
١٠٤ ق + جلّ جلاله.
١٠٥ سورة التحريم ٦٦/٨.
١٠٦ أ: عليه الصلوة والسلام.
١٠٧ سورة ص ٣٨/٤٤.
١٠٨ ح: مدح.
١٠٩ ح – لله تعالى.
١١٠ سورة ق ٥٠/٣٣. ق + صدق الله العظيم.

{14} A section on the difference between *tawba*, *awba* and *ināba*: Imam al-Bushāghirī [c. $4^{th}/10^{th}$ century][30] says regarding the infallibility of the prophets, peace be upon them: *Tawba* is to turn away from the sin; *awba* to turn from the good itself to considering the (divine) support and blessing [in it]; and *ināba* means turning away from everything other than God the Exalted.[31] God the Exalted says: 'O ye who believe, turn to God in sincere repentance. It may be that your Lord will remit from you your evil deeds' [Q 66:8].[32] And when describing Job, peace be upon him, He says: 'How excellent a servant! Truly he turned oft to God' [Q 38:44].[33] God the Exalted thus praises him for (his) submission and consideration of affliction and blessing, as he was patient and grateful to God the Exalted at the time of (both) affliction and blessing. He further says: 'Who feared the All-Merciful in secret and came with a heart turned to Him' [Q 50:33].[34]

30 Muḥammad ibn Yaḥyā al-Bushāghirī, a $4^{th}/10^{th}$ century Māturīdī scholar from Transoxiana. Very little is known about his life, though some of his works have been preserved. For more on his theology, see Mürteza Bedir, "Reason and Revelation. Abū Salama Muḥammad ibn Muḥammad al-Samarqandī (c. $4^{th}/10^{th}$ century), *Jumal uṣūl al-dīn* and Muḥammad ibn Yaḥyā al-Bushāghirī (c. $4^{th}/10^{th}$ century), *Sharḥ Jumal uṣūl al-dīn*", *Māturīdī Theology. A Bilingual Reader*, ed. Lejla Demiri, Philip Dorroll and Dale J. Correa, Tübingen: Mohr Siebeck, 2022, pp. 47-60. This quote must have been from al-Bushāghirī's *Kashf al-ghawāmiḍ fī aḥwāl al-anbiyā'* which has not reached us in its complete form. In an abridgment of it, entitled *al-Muntaqā min 'iṣmat al-anbiyā'* by Nūr al-Dīn al-Ṣābūnī (d. 580/1184), we find only a short definition of *ināba* as 'turning away from people to God, or from one's own attribute to the attributes of God the Exalted' (*al-rujū'u 'an al-khalq ilā Allāh aw min ṣifat nafsihi ilā ṣifāt Allāh Ta'ālā*). See Nūr al-Dīn al-Ṣābūnī, *al-Muntaqā min 'iṣmat al-anbiyā'*, ed. Mehmet Bulut, Istanbul: Nashriyyāt Ri'āsat al-Shu'ūn al-Dīniyya, 2019, p. 141.

31 Earlier Samarqandī spoke of five different types of repentance and how they relate to five degrees of human perfection (see § 6). Here his categorization is threefold, each given a different title. Again, they are listed in an ascending order, from the lowest to the highest spiritual level.

32 A scriptural definition of *tawba*.

33 A scriptural example for *awba*.

34 This is a scriptural proof for *ināba*. In a recent monograph on *tawba* in Islam with a special focus on early Sufism, Atif Khalil, analysing the Qur'anic understanding of the *tawba* points out that 'the Qur'ān employs, alongside *tawba*, two key words, *awba* and *ināba*, to express similar ideas of re/turn; these latter two, however, are never used of God. Moreover, *awba* and *ināba* appear to refer to higher forms of human re/turn, not necessarily from sin or disobedience, and this is why both of these concepts are so closely tied to the re/turn of prophets'. Atif Khalil, *Repentance and the Return to God.* Tawba *in Early Sufism*, Albany, NY: State University of New York, 2018, p. 58.

{١٥} **فصل**: التوبة في صفات الله تعالى توفيقُ العبد ليتوبَ إليه وتثبيتُه على التوبة وقبولُ توبته، إذ التوبةُ من العبد[١١١] الرجوعُ عن طريقِ البُعد إلى طريق القُرب، والمَتابُ المَرجعُ[١١٢]، ومن الله تعالى[١١٣] ترجيعُ[١١٤] آثارِ رحمتِه أو لطفِه[١١٥] إلى عبدِه بعد استحقاقه لعُقوبتِه[١١٦] أو لإبعادِه[١١٧] وإهانتِه. قال الله تعالى[١١٨]: ﴿لَقَدْ تَابَ اللَّهُ[١١٩] عَلَى النَّبِيِّ وَالْمُهَاجِرِينَ﴾ إلى قوله: ﴿ثُمَّ تَابَ عَلَيْهِمْ﴾[١٢٠]، وقال النبي عليه السلام[١٢١]: «ومَنْ[١٢٢] تابَ، تابَ اللهُ[١٢٣] عليه»، أي قَبِلَ اللهُ توبتَه[١٢٤].

{١٦} **فصل**: لتوبة العبد مبدأٌ وأركانٌ وكمالٌ. فالمبدأُ: تبيُّنُ قبْحِ الذنب ووخامةِ[١٢٥] عاقبتِه على القلب[١٢٦].

---

١١١ أ: العبيد.
١١٢ ح – والمتاب المرجع.
١١٣ أ – تعالى.
١١٤ ق + للعباد.
١١٥ ق هـ: للخواص.
١١٦ ق هـ: للعوام.
١١٧ ق + للخواص.
١١٨ ق + عزّ وجلّ.
١١٩ ق هـ: ليتوبوا.
١٢٠ سورة التوبة ٩/١١٧: ﴿لَقَدْ تَابَ اللَّهُ عَلَى النَّبِيِّ وَالْمُهَاجِرِينَ وَالْأَنْصَارِ الَّذِينَ اتَّبَعُوهُ فِي سَاعَةِ الْعُسْرَةِ مِنْ بَعْدِ مَا كَادَ يَزِيغُ قُلُوبُ فَرِيقٍ مِنْهُمْ ثُمَّ تَابَ عَلَيْهِمْ إِنَّهُ بِهِمْ رَءُوفٌ رَحِيمٌ﴾. ق هـ: أي توبتهم عليها.
١٢١ أ: صلى الله عليه وآله وسلم.
١٢٢ ح ق: من.
١٢٣ ح + تعالى.
١٢٤ ح – أي قبل الله توبتَه.
١٢٥ ق هـ: رجل وخم بكسر الخاء ووخم بالتسكين ووخيم ثقيل بيّن الوخامة. من **الصحاح**.
١٢٦ ق هـ: أي ذمامة عاقبته مظهر القلب.

{15} A section: *Tawba* as an attribute of God the Exalted indicates (His) guiding the servant to turn to Him in repentance, making him remain firm on his repentance and accepting his repentance. For the *tawba* of the servant means return from the path of remoteness to the path of nearness;[35] *matāb* indicates that to which one returns;[36] and (the *tawba*) of God the Exalted means [His] making the traits of His mercy and grace return to His servant after he had earned His punishment or His estrangement and His contempt.[37] God the Exalted says, 'God has turned in mercy to the Prophet, and to the Emigrants', up to His statement, 'then He turned to them in mercy' [Q 9:117].[38] And the Prophet, peace be upon him, says: 'God turns to whoever repents',[39] that is God accepts his repentance.[40]

{16} A section: The *tawba* of a servant has a starting point, pillars and completion. The starting point (of repentance) is when the abhorrence of the sin and the disgrace of its outcome become clear to the heart.

35 'The path of remoteness' indicates distance from God, while 'the path of nearness' means nearness to God.

36 Indicating place of return and refuge.

37 *Al-Tawwāb*, the Ever-Relenting, as one of the ninety-nine names of God, indicates for Samarqandī firstly that God facilitates repentance for His servants by guiding them to repent, secondly that He makes them firm in their repentance, and thirdly that He accepts their repentance. So, even the turning of the sinner to God (human *tawba*) is a divine act and mercy, and is encompassed within God's turning to the servant (divine *tawba*).

38 The full Qur'anic verse (9:117) reads: 'God has turned in mercy to the Prophet, and to the Emigrants (*Muhājirīn*) and the Helpers (*Anṣār*) who followed him in the hour of hardship. After the hearts of a party of them had almost swerved aside, then He turned to them in mercy. He is Most Kind and Merciful to them'.

39 Ibn Mājah, *Sunan*, "Iqāmat al-ṣalā", 78, nr. 1134.

40 This double meaning of the *tawba* as 'turning' is explained by the modern Japanese scholar of the Qur'an Toshihiko Izutsu as follows: 'Man "turns" towards God in repentance, and God "turns" towards man with His grace. There is clearly a correlative relationship of "turning" between God and man, and this is reflected in the semantic behavior of the word *tawbah*'. Toshihiko Izutsu, *Ethico-Religious Concepts in the Qur'ān*, Montreal: McGill-Queen's University Press, 2002, p. 110.

وأركانُها: ما ذكرنا من الأمور الثلاثة، وهي: التحسُّر على ما فات، والانقلاع في الحال، والعزمُ على أن لا يعود إلى ذنبه أبداً. وأمّا كمالُها فبالتلافي لما ضيّع أو قصَّر[١٢٧].

{١٧} فإن قيل: إنّ النبي عليه السلام[١٢٨] جعَل نفسَ الندمِ توبةً[١٢٩] بقوله: «النَّدَمُ تَوْبةٌ». قلنا: المراد، والله أعلم، الندم باعثُ التوبة أو أصلُ التوبة، لأنّ التوبةَ اختياريّةٌ داخلةٌ تحت التكليف، وظهورُ الندمِ في القلب جَبْريٌّ[١٣٠]. وقال بعض المشايخ رحمهم الله: معنى الحديث: «النَّدَمُ تَوْبةٌ»، أي[١٣١] معظمُ أركان التوبة، كقوله عليه السلام: «الحَجُّ عَرَفَة»[١٣٢].

{١٨} **فصل**: التوبة إلى الله تعالى واجبةٌ في جميع || الأحوال، ولا يستغني العبدُ عن التوبة إلى أن يزول التكاليف[١٣٣] لوجوهٍ من الدلائل. (١) أحدها: قول الله تعالى: ﴿وَتُوبُوا إِلَى اللَّهِ جَمِيعًا أَيُّهَا الْمُؤْمِنُونَ لَعَلَّكُمْ تُفْلِحُونَ﴾[١٣٤]، والمؤمنون اسمٌ عامٌّ يتناول جميعَ[١٣٥] الأصناف من أهل الشريعة والطريقة والحقيقة. [أ ١٠و]

---

١٢٧ ح – فصل: لتوبة العبد مبدأ وأركان وكمال. فالمبدأُ: تبيُّن قبح الذنب ووخامة عاقبته على القلب. وأركانها: ما ذكرنا من الأمور الثلاثة، وهي: التحسُّر على ما فات، والانقلاع في الحال، والعزمُ على أن لا يعود إلى ذنبه أبداً. وأمّا كمالُها فبالتلافي لما ضيّع أو قصَّر.

١٢٨ أ: عليه الصلوة والسلام.

١٢٩ ق هـ: أي التدارك.

١٣٠ ق هـ: أي بلا واسطة.

١٣١ ق – التوبة أي.

١٣٢ ح – فإن قيل: إنّ النبي عليه السلام جعَل نفس الندم توبةً بقوله: الندمُ توبةٌ. قلنا: المراد والله أعلم الندم باعثُ التوبة أو أصل التوبة، لأنّ التوبة اختياريّة داخلة تحت التكليف، وظهور الندم في القلب جيريٌّ. وقال بعض المشايخ رحمهم الله: معنى الحديث الندم توبة، أي معظم أركان التوبة كقوله عليه السلام: الحجّ عرفة.

١٣٣ ح: يزول من الدنيا.

١٣٤ سورة النور ٢٤/٣١.

١٣٥ ح – جميع.

The pillars (of repentance) are the three principles we mentioned earlier, namely to grieve for what has passed, to desist in the present and determination to not return to the sin ever again. As for the completion (of repentance), it is to make up for what one has neglected or failed in.

{17} If it is claimed: The Prophet, peace be upon him, made regret identical with repentance, with his words, 'Regret is repentance',[41] then we respond: Here the intended meaning is that, and God knows best, regret leads to repentance or it is the root of repentance, for repentance is by choice and within the realm of responsibility (*taklīf*), while the appearance of regret in the heart is a mere compulsion (*jabrī*).[42] One of the shaykhs, may God show mercy to them, said: The meaning of the hadith 'regret is repentance', i.e. (regret) constitutes the major part of the pillars of repentance, is similar to his words, peace be upon him, '*ḥajj* is 'Arafa'.[43]

{18} A section: Turning to God the Exalted in repentance is necessary in all circumstances. *Tawba* is indispensable for a servant as long as the religious obligations last, for several reasons: (1) The words of God the Exalted, 'Turn to God altogether in repentance, O believers, so that you may succeed' [Q 24:31]. The 'believers' is a general noun encompassing all kinds of (believers) from among the people of *sharī'a*, *ṭarīqa* and *ḥaqīqa*.[44]

---

41 Ibn Mājah, *Sunan*, "al-Zuhd", 30, nr. 4393.

42 In other words, regret is by impulse, unlike repentance which is by choice.

43 Journey to the Mount of Arafat is an essential part of pilgrimage, without which the *ḥajj* would be incomplete. For the hadith, see Ibn Mājah, *Sunan*, "al-Manāsik", 57, nr. 3129.

44 Different levels of religiosity from the lowest to the highest.

(٢) الثاني[١٣٦]: قول الله تعالى: ﴿وَاسْتَغْفِرْ لِذَنْبِكَ وَلِلْمُؤْمِنِينَ وَالْمُؤْمِنَاتِ﴾[١٣٧]، والاستغفار هو التوبة. || (٣) الثالث[١٣٨]: قول النبي عليه السلام[١٣٩]: «توبوا إلى الله تعالى، فإنّي أتوب إليه كلَّ يوم مائةَ مرّةٍ». وسيّدُ الخلائق[١٤٠] وزبدةُ العوالم[١٤١] لمّا احتاجَ إلى التوبة فمَن[١٤٢] دونه رُتبةً كان أحوجَ إليها. (٤) الرابع[١٤٣]: العبدُ لا يخلو عن ذنبٍ أو تقصيرٍ أو غفلةٍ أو ملازمةِ مقامٍ نازلٍ عن مقامٍ بعدَه أعلى منه، والوقوفُ في الأوّل قصورٌ وإنْ كان ساعةً، فيجبُ الاستغفارُ عنه. [ح ١٣٥ظ]

{١٩} **فصل**: التوبة من السالك لا تصيرُ[١٤٤] مفتاحاً لمقامات الطريقة حتّى يترُكَ جميعَ الذنوب والقبائح الظاهرة والباطنة، وإن كان التوبة عن بعض المعاصي دونَ البعضِ مقبولةً عند أهل السنّة، لأنّ كُدورةَ القلب واسودادَه بالذنب يمنعُ عن السير إلى الله تعالى.

{٢٠} **فصل في الفرق بين الكافر إذا تاب والعاصي إذا تاب**[١٤٥]. نقول: الكافر إذا صحَّ إيمانُه وإسلامُه يُغفَر له ما قد سلف، وإسلامُه يَجُبُّ[١٤٦] ما قبلَه ويهدمُ ما فرّط[١٤٧] لقول الله تعالى: || ﴿قُلْ لِلَّذِينَ كَفَرُوا إِنْ يَنْتَهُوا يُغْفَرْ لَهُمْ مَا قَدْ سَلَفَ﴾[١٤٨]، [أ ١٠ظ]

---

١٣٦ ح: والثاني.
١٣٧ سورة محمّد ١٩/٤٧.
١٣٨ ح: والثالث.
١٣٩ أ: صلى الله عليه واله وسلم.
١٤٠ ح: الخلق.
١٤١ ح – وزبدةُ العوالم.
١٤٢ ح + كان.
١٤٣ ق: والرابع.
١٤٤ ح ق: يصير.
١٤٥ ح هـ: مطلب في الفرق بين توبة الكافر وبين توبة العاصي.
١٤٦ ح: يهدم.
١٤٧ ح – ويهدم ما فرّط.
١٤٨ سورة الأنفال ٣٨/٨.

(2) The words of God the Exalted, 'And ask forgiveness for your sin and for believing men and for believing women' [Q 47:19]. So asking forgiveness is repentance. (3) The words of the Prophet, peace be upon him, 'Turn to God the Exalted in repentance. Truly, I turn to Him in repentance a hundred times a day'.[45] Since the master of all created beings and epitome of all worlds felt the need to repent, those below him in status are even more so in need of it. (4) A servant cannot be free from sin, shortcoming or holding on a lower station when the next station is higher, for pausing at the prior (station) even if it be for a moment is a shortcoming, and therefore requires asking forgiveness for it.

{19} A section: The repentance of a wayfarer on the spiritual path cannot open the gates to the stations of the *ṭarīqa* until all sins and evil acts, be they external or internal, are abandoned. This is so, even though repenting for some sinful acts without repenting for some others is valid, according to the Ahl al-Sunna. For the impurity of the heart and its blackening with sin obstruct the journey on the path to God the Exalted.

{20} A section on the difference between the repentance of the unbeliever and the repentance of the (believing) sinner. We say: When the unbeliever truly becomes a believer and accepts Islam, he is forgiven for all that has passed before. His conversion to Islam cuts off entirely what has passed before and wipes out what has preceded, due to the words of God the Exalted: 'Tell those who disbelieve that if they desist, that which is past will be forgiven for them' [Q 8:38].

45 See Muslim, *Ṣaḥīḥ*, "al-Dhikr wa-l-du'ā' wa-l-tawba wa-l-istighfār", 12, nr. 7034; Baghawī, *Maṣābīḥ*, vol. 2, p. 164, nr. 1664.

وقال النبي عليه السلام[١٤٩]: «الإسلامُ يَجُبُّ ما قبلَه»، أي يقطع، وفي رواية: «الإسلامُ[١٥٠] يَهْدِمُ ما قبله، والهجرةُ[١٥١] تَهْدِمُ ما[١٥٢] قبلها، والحجُّ يَهْدِمُ ما قبله».

{٢١} والعاصي لا يكمل[١٥٣] توبتُه ما لم يُرضِ خُصَمائَه بقدر الإمكان ويتلافَ[١٥٤] ما فوَّت وإن كانت[١٥٥] ماهيّةُ التوبة لا يتوقّف عليهما على ما ذكرنا[١٥٦]. وإنّما كان كذلك، لأنّ الضعفاءَ يُسَهَّلُ || عليهم كيلا ينفروا، والأقوياءَ يُشدَّدُ عليهم [ح ١٣٦و] لِيَسْعَوا إلى المنازل الرفيعة. || قال النبي عليه السلام[١٥٧]: «حسناتُ الأبرار سيّئاتُ [ق ٥١ظ] المقرَّبين»[١٥٨].

{٢٢} فالكافر إذا قال مرّةً واحدةً عن صدق قلبه مخلصاً: لا إله إلّا الله محمّد رسول الله، وتبرّأ من[١٥٩] جميع الأديان الباطلة خرجَ عن ذنوبه بأسرها، وصار كيوم ولدتْه أمُّه، وطابَ[١٦٠] جميعُ أمواله التي كسبها بأسبابٍ فاسدةٍ، ويرضي اللهُ تعالى جميعَ خصمائِه بفضله ورحمته، ويُغنيه عمّا ذكرنا من التلافي[١٦١] والقضاء[١٦٢]،

---

١٤٩ أ: صلى الله عليه واله وسلم؛ ح: صلى الله تعالى عليه وسلم. ح هـ: مطلب في أن الإسلام يجب ما قبله والهجرة تهدم ما قبله والحج ما قبله.
١٥٠ ح – الإسلام.
١٥١ ق هـ: الهجرة هجرتان. هجرة كان فريضة في زمن الرسول، وأمّا في زماننا ما بقي الهجرة لقوله عليه السلام: لا هجرة بعد الفتح. وأمّا في زماننا الهجرة الثانية باقية وهي الهجرة من السيّئات لقوله عليه السلام: الهاجر من السيّئات. والله أعلم.
١٥٢ أ + كان.
١٥٣ ح: ما تكمل.
١٥٤ ح: ويتدارك.
١٥٥ ح: كان.
١٥٦ ح – على ما ذكرنا.
١٥٧ أ: عليه الصلوة والسلام.
١٥٨ ح – قال النبي عليه السلام: حسنات الأبرار سيّات المقرّبين.
١٥٩ أ: عن.
١٦٠ ح: وطابت.
١٦١ ق هـ: أي تدارك.
١٦٢ ح – ولغُنية عمّا ذكرنا من التلافي والقضاء.

And the Prophet, peace be upon him, says: 'Embracing Islam cuts off entirely what has passed before',[46] i.e. deletes [all previous sins]. And according to another narration, (the Prophet says): 'Embracing Islam wipes out what precedes it, the *hijra* wipes out what precedes it and the *ḥajj* wipes out what precedes it'.[47]

{21} As for the (believing) sinner, his repentance will be incomplete until he makes amends to those he has wronged as much as he can and until he makes up what has passed, even though the very essence of repentance does not depend on these two, as we have indicated (above). This is so, in order to make things easy for the weak ones (in faith) lest they run away[48] and to be strict toward the strong ones (in faith) so they may strive for the elevated dwellings.[49] The Prophet, peace be upon him, said: 'The virtues of the pious are the faults of those drawn near to God'.[50]

{22} Regarding the unbeliever, once he, confirming with his heart, sincerely says, 'There is no god but God and Muḥammad is the Messenger of God', and renounces all wrong beliefs, he is free from all his sins entirely, becomes (sinless) as on the day his mother gave birth to him, all his properties that he has acquired through wrong means become lawful, and God the Exalted out of His kindness and mercy makes amends to all those he has wronged and renders him free from the need to make up [what has passed] which we have mentioned.

46 Aḥmad ibn Ḥanbal, *Musnad*, vol. 29, p. 315.

47 See Muslim, *Ṣaḥīḥ*, "al-Īmān", 53, nr. 336.

48 Lest they keep their distance from God. As Samarqandī explained earlier, repentance indicates nearness to God, while sinful state means distance from Him.

49 In the heavenly Garden.

50 Quite often this saying is attributed to the Prophet. See, for instance, Abū Ḥāmid al-Ghazālī, *Sirr al-ʿālamayn wa-kashf mā fī l-dārayn*, in *Majmūʿat rasāʾil al-Imām al-Ghazālī*, ed. Ibrāhīm Amīn Muḥammad, Cairo: al-Maktaba al-Tawfīqiyya, (n.d.), pp. 478-506, at p. 502. Sometimes, however, it is quoted as an anonymous saying of wisdom. See al-Ḥakīm al-Tirmidhī, *Riyāḍat al-nafs*, ed. Ibrāhīm Shams al-Dīn, Beirut: Dār al-Kutub al-ʿIlmiyya, 1426/2005, p. 26; Abū Ṭālib al-Makkī, *Qūt al-qulūb fī muʿāmalat al-maḥbūb wa-waṣf ṭarīq al-murīd ilā maqām al-tawḥīd*, ed. Maḥmūd Ibrāhīm Muḥammad al-Raḍwānī, Cairo: Maktabat Dār al-Turāth, 1422/2001, vol. 2, p. 623. In some sources, it is also attributed to some early sufi authorities, such as Abū Saʿīd al-Kharrāz (see Abū Bakr al-Khaṭīb al-Baghdādī, *Tārīkh madīnat al-salām*, ed. Bashshār ʿAwwād Maʿrūf, Beirut: Dār al-Gharb al-Islāmī, 1422/2001, vol. 5, p. 456) or al-Junayd (see Abū ʿAbd Allāh al-Qurṭubī, *al-Jāmiʿ li-aḥkām al-Qurʾān*, ed. ʿAbd Allāh ibn ʿAbd al-Muḥsin al-Turkī, Beirut: Muʾassasat al-Risāla, 1427/2006, vol. 1, p. 460).

﴿وَلَهُ الْحُكْمُ﴾[١٦٣]، و﴿لَا يُسْأَلُ عَمَّا يَفْعَلُ وَهُمْ يُسْأَلُونَ﴾[١٦٤].

{٢٣} **فصل**[١٦٥]: التوبة التي هي[١٦٦] أصعَبُ أقسام التوبة على السالك توبةُ الاستقامة، وهي رعايةُ البَهيمِيّاتِ والسبُعيّات والشيطانيّات والملكيّات والرُبوبيّات على قانون العقل والشرع، والتحرُّزُ[١٦٧] عن الإفراط[١٦٨] والتفريط[١٦٩] فيها، والثباتُ على الحدِّ الوسط[١٧٠]، والاستغفارُ عمّا وُجد منه إفراطٌ أو[١٧١] تفريطٌ || فيها في [أ ١١و] عمره. وقال نبيُّنا[١٧٢] صلّى الله تعالى عليه وسلّم[١٧٣]: «شيَّبَتْني سورةُ هود»[١٧٤]. قيل: أي من شدَّة رعاية أمر[١٧٥] الاستقامة المذكور في قوله تعالى[١٧٦]: ﴿فَاسْتَقِمْ كَمَا أُمِرْتَ وَمَنْ تَابَ مَعَكَ وَلَا تَطْغَوْا إِنَّهُ بِمَا تَعْمَلُونَ بَصِيرٌ﴾[١٧٧].

{٢٤} وقال المشايخ رحمهم الله[١٧٨]: الثباتُ على النَّمَط الأوسط أدقُّ من الشَّعْر وأحدُّ من السيف، ولذا أمر اللهُ تعالى بالدعاء وسُؤالِ الاستقامة في مُفتَتَح كتابه في[١٧٩] قوله:

---

١٦٣ سورة القصص ٢٨/٧٠. ح – ﴿وَلَهُ الْحُكْمُ﴾.
١٦٤ سورة الأنبياء ٢١/٢٣.
١٦٥ ح هـ: مطلب في أن أصعب أقسام التوبة توبة الاستقامة.
١٦٦ ح – التوبة التي هي.
١٦٧ ح – التجرّد.
١٦٨ ق هـ: أي الغلو في الأشياء.
١٦٩ ق هـ: أي التقصير.
١٧٠ ح – الأوسط.
١٧١ ح: و.
١٧٢ ح: قال النبيّ.
١٧٣ أ: صلى الله عليه واله وسلم.
١٧٤ أ ق + عليه السلام.
١٧٥ ق: الأمر.
١٧٦ ح: وقيل من شدّة رعاية أمر الاستقامة قول الله تعالى.
١٧٧ سورة هود ١١/١١٢.
١٧٨ ح + تعالى. ح هـ: مطلب قال المشايخ الثبات على النمط الأوسط أدقّ من الشعر وأحدّ من السيف.
١٧٩ ح – في.

'And His is the judgement' [Q 28:70] and 'He cannot be questioned for anything He does, but they will be questioned' [Q 21:23].

{23} A section: The most difficult kind of repentance for the wayfarer is the repentance of integrity (*istiqāma*), which is to watch over the bestial, devilish, angelic and lordly traits following reason and religious law, to guard against excessiveness (*ifrāṭ*) and deficiency (*tafrīṭ*) in these (traits), to keep firmly to the middle line, and to seek forgiveness for whatever excessive or deficient things may have proceeded from him throughout his life. Our Prophet, may God the Exalted bless him and grant him peace, said: 'Sūra Hūd has made me age'.[51] It is said: This is so because of the difficulty of observing the commandment of integrity, mentioned in the words of (God) the Exalted: 'So keep to the right course as you have been commanded, together with those who have turned to God with you. Do not overstep the limits, for He sees everything you do' [Q 11:112].

{24} The sufi masters, may God show them mercy, said: Keeping firmly to the middle way is thinner than a hair and sharper than a sword. It is because of this that God the Exalted commanded (us) to pray and ask for integrity in the opening of His Book, with His words:

51 The hadith is reported as *shayyabatnī Hūd* (Hūd has made me age) in Tirmidhī, *Sunan*, "Tafsīr al-Qur'ān", 56, nr. 3609.

﴿اهْدِنَا[١٨٠] || الصِّرَاطَ الْمُسْتَقِيمَ﴾[١٨١]، وأَوْجَب النبيُّ عليه الصلاة والسلام[١٨٢] قراءَةَ الفاتحة في كلِّ صلاة لهذا، والله[١٨٣] أعلم. فمن كانت محافظتُه لمقام الاستقامة أقوى كان مُرُورُه على الصراط في الآخرة أسهل. ولصعوبة تحصيل هذا المقام[١٨٤] قلنا: التوبةُ واجبةٌ دائماً، ولذا قال النبي عليه السلام[١٨٥]: «اسْتَقِيمُوا ولَنْ تُحْصُوا». والله المُيسِّرُ لكُلِّ عسيرٍ[١٨٦]. [ح ١٣٦ظ]

{٢٥} **فصل**[١٨٧]: توبة الإذابة يحتاج إليها أهلُ الإرادة[١٨٨] في مبدأ حالهم[١٨٩]، إذ زجَّوْا[١٩٠] مُدّةً مديدةً من أوقات عمرهم في الغفلات والمعاصي[١٩١] والتنعُّمات على الهوى والطبع، فصفاؤُهم الكاملُ يتوقَّف على إذابَتِهم أبدانَهم بالمجاهدات، ورياضةِ نفوسِهم الأَبِيَّة[١٩٢]، وإظهارِ التَّرَحاتِ[١٩٣] بعد الفَرَحاتِ[١٩٤]، والبكاءِ في الخَلَوات بعد مجاهرة الضحك بين أرباب البطالات[١٩٥].

---

١٨٠ ق هـ: أي ثبتنا. ح هـ: مطلب في أنّ الله تعالى أمر عباده في مفتتح كتابه الكريم بالاستقامة وطلب الهداية على الصراط المستقيم.

١٨١ سورة الفاتحة ٦/١.

١٨٢ ق – الصلاة والسلام؛ ح: صلى الله تعالى عليه وسلم.

١٨٣ ح + تعالى.

١٨٤ ح: والصعوبة تحصل فى هذا المقام.

١٨٥ أ: صلى الله عليه واله وسلم.

١٨٦ The text of the *risāla* in the MS Kastamonu (ق) comes to an end here, and there begins another text which includes a discussion on the heart (*qalb*), the need for its purification, character traits that are perilous and ways to get rid of them.

١٨٧ ح هـ: مطلب في بيان التوبة المقبولة.

١٨٨ ح + الايمان.

١٨٩ ح: جالهم.

١٩٠ ح هـ: أي قطعوا.

١٩١ ح + والنعمات.

١٩٢ ح: الأَبَويّة.

١٩٣ ح: الترآحآت.

١٩٤ ح: الفرآحآت.

١٩٥ ح: البطلات.

'Guide us to the straight path' [Q 1:6]. Likewise, the Prophet, blessings and peace be upon him, enjoined (us) to recite (Sūra) Fātiḥa in every prayer, due to this. And God knows best. The stronger one's observance of the station of integrity the easier will be his passing over the Bridge in the hereafter. Since it is difficult to attain this station, we have said: Repentance is necessary at all times. Hence the statement of the Prophet, peace be upon him: 'Be righteous and you will not be able to count [God's blessings]'.[52] And God is the Giver of ease for all difficulties.

{25} A section: An exhaustive repentance is needed for the seekers (of the path) at the beginning of their state,[53] for they have spent a long time of their lives in heedlessness, sinfulness, and the enjoyment of desires and pleasures of nature. So, their complete purification is dependent on their exhausting their bodies with strivings, exercising spiritual practices on their proud egos, finding rest after joyful delights, and crying in seclusion after laughing loudly in the midst of people of futile pursuits.

52 Ibn Mājah, *Sunan*, "al-Ṭahāra", 4, nr. 290.

53 These are novices on the path and their initial repentance when entering the sufi path of spiritual purification. See § 10.

{٢٦} **فصل**[١٩٦]: قال الجُنيد رحمه الله: التوبة أن لا تنْسَى ذنبَك، وقال عارفٌ للجُنيد رحمه الله: لا، بل التوبة أن تنْسَى ذنبَك. وقال || [أبو] بكر بن إسحاق [أ ١١ظ] الكلاباذي البخاري[١٩٧] رحمه الله في التوفيق بينهما وجهاً حسناً في **كتاب التعرُّف**. وشرحُ ذلك ما نقول[١٩٨]: إنّ السالكَ في مبدأ أحواله والسير إلى الله تعالى || يجب عليه أن لا ينْسَى ذنوبَه، قال الله تعالى: ﴿وَمَنْ أَظْلَمُ مِمَّنْ ذُكِّرَ [ح ١٣٧و] بِآيَاتِ رَبِّهِ فَأَعْرَضَ عَنْهَا وَنَسِيَ مَا قَدَّمَتْ يَدَاهُ﴾[١٩٩]، فحقيقٌ عليه أن يُعدِّدَ[٢٠٠] ذنوبَه في الخَلَوات مع الله تعالى الكريمِ العفوِّ الستّارِ[٢٠١]، ويبكيَ عليها ويعتذرَ، فإنّه تعالى[٢٠٢] يُحِبُّ العذْرَ، ويَضعَ وجهَه على التراب ساجداً، ويقولَ في سجوده متضرِّعاً: يا ربِّ! عبدُك الآبقُ رجعَ إلى بابك، عبدُك[٢٠٣] الجافي رجعَ إلى جنابك، وقد أمرتَ عبادَك أن يتجاوَزُوا ويعْفُوا عن المُسِيئِينَ حيث قلتَ: ﴿فَمَنْ عَفَا وَأَصْلَحَ فَأَجْرُهُ عَلَى اللهِ﴾[٢٠٤]، وأوّلُ راضي سُنّةٍ مَنْ وضعَها، وقلتَ: ﴿وَأَنْ تَصَدَّقُوا خَيْرٌ لَكُمْ﴾[٢٠٥]، وأمرتَ نبيَّك عليه الصلاة والسلام[٢٠٦] بالعفو والاستغفار والشفاعة بقولك: ﴿خُذِ الْعَفْوَ وَأْمُرْ بِالْعُرْفِ﴾[٢٠٧]، وقولك: ﴿فَاعْفُ عَنْهُمْ وَاسْتَغْفِرْ لَهُمْ﴾[٢٠٨]، وقولك: ﴿وَاسْتَغْفِرْ لِذَنْبِكَ وَلِلْمُؤْمِنِينَ وَالْمُؤْمِنَاتِ﴾[٢٠٩]،

١٩٦ ح هـ: مطلب قال الجنيد التوبة أن لا تنسى ذنبك وقال العارف للجنيد لا بل أن تنسى ذنبك.

١٩٧ ح – الكلاباذي البخاري.

١٩٨ ح – في كتاب التعرُّف، وشرحُ ذلك ما نقول.

١٩٩ سورة الكهف ٥٧/١٨.

٢٠٠ ح: يَعُدَّ.

٢٠١ ح: الكريم الستار العفو الغفار.

٢٠٢ أ ق – تعالى.

٢٠٣ ح: وعبدك.

٢٠٤ سورة الشعراء ٤٠/٤٢.

٢٠٥ سورة البقرة ٢٨٠/٢. ح – وأوّل راضي سُنّةٍ من وضعها، وقلتَ: ﴿وَأَنْ تَصَدَّقُوا خَيْرٌ لَكُمْ﴾.

٢٠٦ ح: عليه السلام.

٢٠٧ سورة الأعراف ١٩٩/٧.

٢٠٨ سورة آل عمران ١٥٩/٣.

٢٠٩ سورة محمّد ١٩/٤٧.

{26} A section: Al-Junayd, may God show him mercy, said: 'Repentance is not to forget your sin'; and a man who knows (God) told al-Junayd, may God show him mercy: 'No, instead repentance is to forget your sin'. [Abū] Bakr [Muḥammad] ibn Isḥāq al-Kalābādhī al-Bukhārī [d. 380/990], may God show him mercy, mentioned a beautiful point reconciling the two in (his) *Kitāb al-Ta'arruf* ('Book of Acquaintance').[54] And we explain it as follows: It is necessary for the wayfarer not to forget his sins at the beginning of his states and his journey to God the Exalted, as God the Exalted says: 'Who could be more wrong than he who has been reminded of the revelations of his Lord, yet turns away from them and forgets what his hands send forward (to the Judgment)' [Q 18:57]. So it is apt that he should reckon his sins time after time in his solitary moments with God the Exalted, the Generous, the Effacer of sins, the Concealer, and that he should weep over them and ask forgiveness for his sins; as He the Exalted loves to forgive. He should also place his face on earth prostrating and say in prostration imploring: 'O Lord, Your fugitive servant has returned to Your door; Your estranged servant has returned to Your presence. You indeed command Your servants to excuse and pardon offenders, as You say: "But whosoever pardons and amends, his reward is due from God" [Q 42:40], and the first to approve a norm is the one who has laid it down.[55] As You further say: "And that you remit the debt as almsgiving would be better for you" [Q 2:280]. You also ordered Your Prophet, blessing and peace be upon him, to pardon, ask for forgiveness and intercede with Your words: "Keep to forgiveness, and enjoin kindness" [Q 7:199], and Your words: "So pardon them and ask forgiveness for them" [Q 3:159] and "Ask forgiveness for your sin, and for believing men and believing women" [Q 47:19].

54 In fact, Kalābādhī attributes the opposite opinion to al-Junayd, as he writes: 'Al-Junayd was asked, "What is repentance?" He replied: "It is the forgetting of one's sin." Sahl, being asked the same question, said: "It consists of not forgetting one's sin." This saying of Al-Junayd means, that the sweetness of such an act so entirely departs from the heart, that there remains in the conscience not a trace of it, and one is then as though one had never known it.' Abū Bakr al-Kalābādhī, *The Doctrine of the Ṣūfis (Kitāb al-Ta'arruf li-madhhab ahl al-taṣawwuf)*, trans. Arthur John Arberry, Cambridge: Cambridge University Press, 1935, pp. 82-3. For the Arabic original, see Abū Bakr al-Kalābādhī, *Kitāb al-Ta'arruf li-madhhab ahl al-taṣawwuf*, ed. Arthur John Arberry, Cairo: Maktabat al-Khānjī, 1415/1994 (1st ed. 1352/1933), p. 64.

55 Since God has commanded people to forgive one another, it is more appropriate that He, as the Law-Giver, practices Himself this rule first.

فتجاوَزْ عن قبيحِ ما عندي بجميل ما عندكَ، يا كريم! وكيف لا تعفُو عمَّن أناب إليك ونَدِمَ على مخالفاته[٢١٠]، وأنت أكرم الأكرمين وأرحم الراحمين! وقُلْ بلسانٍ خاشعٍ[٢١١] في جَوْفِ الليالي وفي الأسحار[٢١٢] عند تحرُّر قطرات[٢١٣] الدموع[٢١٤] || [ح ١٣٧ظ] على وَجَناتِك[٢١٥]: اللّهمَّ اغفرْ لي ما سَلَفَ من الذنوب، واعْصمني عنها فيما بقي من حياتي[٢١٦]، || يا جوادُ، يا كريمُ، يا رحيمُ! [أ ١٢و]

{٢٧} فعند هذه التضرّعات والإنابات[٢١٧] نرجو أن يُبدِّلَ اللهُ[٢١٨] سيّئاتِكَ حسناتٍ ويُنْسِيَ قبائحَك على الإنس والجنّ والملائكة وسائر الخلق. قال الله تعالى: ﴿فَأُولَئِكَ يُبَدِّلُ اللَّهُ سَيِّئَاتِهِمْ حَسَنَاتٍ﴾[٢١٩]. فأمّا[٢٢٠] السالك إذا صار واصلًا ودخل في مقام المحبّة والمشاهدةِ فحقيقٌ عليه أن لا يَذكر سيّئاتِه، إذ ذِكْرُ الجفاءِ في مقام الصفاء جفاءٌ[٢٢١]، وذِكْرُ الوَحشة بين يدي الملِك وَحشةٌ.

{٢٨} **فصل**[٢٢٢]: تعييرُ الخطَّائين[٢٢٣] وتقريعُهم حرامٌ لقول الخضر عليه[٢٢٤] الصلاة والسلام[٢٢٥] في وصيّته لموسى عليه الصلاة والسلام[٢٢٦] عند فراقه:

٢١٠ ح: مُخاَلَفته.
٢١١ ح – خاشعٍ.
٢١٢ ح: اَسْحاَرِهِ.
٢١٣ ح: عند سَيَلاَبِ.
٢١٤ ح: دُمُوعِكَ.
٢١٥ ح هـ: الوجانة ما ارتفع من الخدّين.
٢١٦ أ ح: حيوتى.
٢١٧ ح – والإنابات.
٢١٨ ح + تعالى.
٢١٩ سورة الفرقان ٢٥/٧٠.
٢٢٠ ح: وأمّا.
٢٢١ ح: خباء.
٢٢٢ ح هـ: مطلب في بيت وغير تقي يأمر الناس بالتقى طبيب يداوي الناس وهو مريض.
٢٢٣ ح: الخاطئين.
٢٢٤ ح: عليهم.
٢٢٥ ح – الصلاة والسلام.
٢٢٦ ح: عليه السلام.

So do forgive the ugly in me with the beauty in You, O Generous! And how would You, being the Most Generous of the generous and Most Merciful of the merciful, not pardon the one who has turned repentantly to You and regretted his offenses?' And in the middle of the night and a little before daybreak say with a humble voice while drops of tears run free over your cheeks: 'O my God, forgive me for all the sins of the past and protect me from them in what is left of my life, O Magnanimous, O Generous, O Merciful!'

{27} Upon these entreaties and turning repentantly (to God), we hope that God will change your evil deeds to good deeds and cause your ugly deeds against humans, jinn, angels and other creatures to be forgotten.[56] God the Exalted says: 'As for such, God will change their evil deeds to good deeds' [Q 25:70]. And when the wayfarer reaches [the heights of his spiritual journey] and enters the station of love (*maḥabba*) and witnessing (*mushāhada*), it is apt that he should not mention his evil deeds, for the mention of estrangement at the station of reciprocal purity and sincerity of love is coarseness, and the mention of alienation before the king is alienation.

{28} A section: It is impermissible to upbraid and scold those who commit many errors,[57] due to the words of Khiḍr, blessings and peace be upon him, in his counsel to Moses, blessings and peace be upon him, at the time of his separation:

56 Or: make humans, jinn, angels and other creatures forget your ugly deeds.
57 Or: those who constantly commit errors.

«لا تُعَيِّر أحداً على خطيئته، وابْك على خطِيئتك، يا ابن[٢٢٧] عمران»! كما قيل على سفيان رحمه الله:

وغيرُ تقيٍّ يأمرُ الناسَ بالتقى　　طبيبٌ يداوي الناسَ وهو مريض

فأجابهم سفيان رحمه الله:

اعملْ بعلمي[٢٢٨] وإن قصَّرتُ في عملي　　ينفعْكَ علمي ولا يضرُرْكَ تقصيري[٢٢٩]

{٢٩} والملامة بعد التوبة لا تجوز أيضاً لقول نبيّنا عليه الصلاة والسلام: «احتجَّ آدم وموسى عليهما السلام، فحَجَّ آدمُ على موسى عليهما السلام»، على ما روي في **المصابيح والصحيح**. وقال[٢٣٠] الله تعالى لداود عليه السلام: || «بشِّر التائبين كي لا[٢٣١] يقنطوا، وأنذر الصدّيقين كي لا[٢٣٢] يُعجَبُوا». [ح ١٣٨و]

٢٢٧ ح: بن.
٢٢٨ ح: بعملى.
٢٢٩ أ – كما قيل على سفيان رحمه الله: وغيرُ تقيٍّ يأمرُ الناسَ بالتقى طبيبٌ يداوي الناسَ وهو مريض، فأجابهم سفيان رحمه الله: اعملْ بعلمي وإن قصَّرتُ في عملي ينفعْكَ علمي ولا يضرُرْكَ تقصيري.
٢٣٠ ح – نبيّنا عليه الصلاة والسلام: احتجّ آدم وموسى عليهما السلام فحجّ آدمُ على موسى عليهما السلام، على ما روي في **المصابيح والصحيح**. وقال.
٢٣١ أ ح: كيلا.
٢٣٢ أ ح: كيلا.

'Never upbraid anyone for his error; instead weep over your own error, O son of 'Imrān!'[58] Likewise, Sufyān [ibn 'Uyayna (d. 198/815)], may God show him mercy, was told:

> 'An unrighteous person commanding people with righteousness; (just like) a doctor treating people while he himself is ill!'[59]

Sufyān, may God show him mercy, responded:

> 'Act according to my knowledge, even if I may fall short in my own deeds; my knowledge will be useful to you, while my shortcoming will not hurt you'.[60]

{29} Reproach after repentance is also not permitted, due to the words of our Prophet, blessings and peace be upon him: 'Adam and Moses, peace be upon them both, adduced an argument (in self-defense), and Adam overcame Moses, peace be upon them both, with (his) argument',[61] according to what was narrated in *al-Maṣābīḥ*[62] and *al-Ṣaḥīḥ*.[63] God the Exalted said to David, peace be upon him: 'Announce glad tidings to those who repent lest they despair, and give warning to those who are righteous lest they become conceited'.[64]

58 This report appears with some variations in wording, for instance, in Sulaymān ibn Muqātil, *Tafsīr*, ed. 'Abd Allāh Maḥmūd Shaḥāta, Beirut: Mu'assasat al-Tārīkh al-'Arabī, 1423/2002, vol. 3, p. 49; Abū Bakr al-Bayhaqī, *al-Jāmi' li-shu'ab al-īmān*, ed. Mukhtār Aḥmad al-Nadwī, Riyadh: Maktabat al-Rushd, 1423/2003, vol. 9, p. 65.

59 The verse is from a well-known poem by an anonymous poet. See Abū Manṣūr 'Abd al-Malik al-Tha'ālibī, *Khāṣṣ al-khāṣṣ*, ed. Ḥasan al-Amīn, Beirut: Dār Maktabat al-Ḥayāt, (n.d.), p. 35.

60 Quoted in Abū Bakr al-Bayhaqī, *al-Madkhal ilā l-sunan al-kubrā*, ed. Muḥammad Ḍiyā' al-Raḥmān al-A'ẓamī, Kuwait: Dār al-Khulafā', (n.d.), pp. 446-7.

61 In a lengthy narration Adam wins the argument by raising the question of *qadar*: How can one blame him for having done an act which God had predetermined (*qaddarahu*) in pre-eternity?

62 Baghawī, *Maṣābīḥ*, vol. 1, pp. 132-3, nr. 60.

63 The hadith is narrated in various reports in Bukhārī, *Ṣaḥīḥ*, "al-Qadar", 11, nr. 6695; Muslim, *Ṣaḥīḥ*, "al-Qadar", 2, nr. 6912-5.

64 This is a summarized statement found in a narration describing a dialogue between God and the prophet David, for instance, quoted by the 9th century sufi exegete Sahl al-Tustarī (d. 283/896). See Sahl ibn 'Abd Allāh al-Tustarī, *Tafsīr al-Tustarī*, ed. Ṭāhā 'Abd al-Ra'ūf Sa'd and Sa'd Ḥasan Muḥammad 'Alī, Cairo: Dār al-Ḥaram li-l-Turāth, 1425/2004, pp. 141-2; Sahl b. 'Abd Allāh al-Tustarī, *Tafsīr al-Tustarī*, trans. Annabel Keeler and Ali Keeler, Louisville, KY: Fons Vitae, 2011, p. 64.

{٣٠} **فصل**: علامةُ قبولِ توبةِ العاصي برُودةُ مجالسةِ[٢٣٣] أقران[٢٣٤] السوءِ على قلبه، وحصولُ التوفيقِ على المجاهدات والرياضاتِ، والتحسُّرُ والبكاءُ على ما زَجَّى عمرَه في الزلّات، واختيارُ مصاحبةِ أهل العلم والتقوى والألباب[٢٣٥]، والملازمةُ على الوظائف والأوراد[٢٣٦] آناءَ الليل وأطرافَ النهار.

{٣١} **فصل**: التائب الصادق حقٌّ[٢٣٧] عليه هجرانُ دواعي المخالفات والجَفَوات، والتجنُّبُ عن مخالطة أهلها، والتحرّزُ عن إيشاع[٢٣٨] المعاصي[٢٣٩] || وتَخيُّلِها[٢٤٠] [أ ١٢ظ] وقبولِ خواطرها الباعثةِ للنفس عليها[٢٤١]. فيجب عليه معالجةُ الضدِّ بالضدِّ فيغلّبُ على قلبه دواعي الموافقات، والاختلاطُ[٢٤٢] بأهل الخير والتقوى، واستماعُ الحِكَم والمواعظ ومطالعتُها[٢٤٣] وتخيُّلُها[٢٤٤]، واستماعُ ذكر الصالحين، وقبولُ خواطرِ الحقِّ إلى أن يتعوّدَ نفسه بها. فإنّ الخيرَ عادةٌ والشرَّ عادةٌ، والنفس معتادةٌ، فما عوَّدتَها به تَتعوَّد[٢٤٥]. واللّٰه الموفِّق والمرشد والمُسَدِّدُ بكرمه[٢٤٦].

٢٣٣ ح – مجالسة.
٢٣٤ ح: قرناء.
٢٣٥ ح – والألباب.
٢٣٦ ح: الاورآد والوظايف.
٢٣٧ ح: واجب.
٢٣٨ أ: اشياع، ح – إيشاع.
٢٣٩ ح: العاصى.
٢٤٠ ح: وتخلّيها.
٢٤١ ح – وقبول خواطرها الباعثةِ للنفس عليها.
٢٤٢ ح: واخطلات.
٢٤٣ ح: ومطالعاتها.
٢٤٤ ح – وتخيّلها.
٢٤٥ ح – فإنّ الخير عادةٌ والشرّ عادةٌ، والنفس معتادةٌ، فما عوّدتَها به تَتعوَّد.
٢٤٦ أ + تمّت الرسالة على يد العبد الضعيف الراجي رحمة ربّه عبد الوهّاب بن محمود بن أحمد المراغي عفا الله عنه وعن جميع المؤمنين والمؤمنات والمسلمين والمسلمات. والحمد لله ربّ العالمين، والعاقبة للمتقين، ولا عدوان إلّا على الظالمين.
ح + كتبه الفقير الحقير المعترف بالعجز والتقصير عبد الرحمن الداعي في الجامع الكبير عفى الله تعالى عنه الذنب الكبير والنقير.

{30} A section: Indications that the repentance of the sinner is accepted are as follows: coldness of the heart towards keeping company with associates of evil, successfully accomplishing strivings and spiritual exercises, feeling grief and weeping for having spent one's life in lapses, preference for accompanying people of knowledge, the God-fearing and the people of understanding, and incessantly practicing spiritual duties and litanies during the hours of the night and at the two ends of the day.[65]

{31} A section: It is incumbent upon a truthful penitent to abandon whatever tempts him to opposition and estrangement, to avoid mingling with people (of temptation), and to guard against openly committing transgressions,[66] imagining them, or entertaining any thoughts of them that would incite the soul to commit them. A treatment with the opposite is required for such a person so that the incentives to compliance are made to overcome his heart. He should further mix with people of goodness and piety, and should listen, read and reflect on words of wisdom and exhortations. He should also listen to the commemoration of the righteous ones and consider truthful thoughts so that he may habituate himself to them [i.e. such thoughts]. Good is a habit and evil is a habit, and the soul is habituated; whatever you habituate it with, it will be habituated with that thing.[67] And with His Generosity God is the Provider of success, guidance and right direction.

65 At the beginning and end of the day, i.e. in the morning and evening. For a similar expression, see Q 20:130, 'Therefore (O Prophet), bear with what they say, and celebrate the praise of your Lord, before the rising of the sun and before its setting. And glorify Him some hours of the night and at the two ends of the day, so that you may find contentment'.

66 Or: disclosing (past) transgressions, and making them public, as Samarqandī warned against doing this above.

67 Here Samarqandī notes that the human being is a creature of habit and therefore it is important to adopt good habits and avoid bad ones. The emphasis being on the importance of training the soul, the message is clear: no one is evil by nature. Hence the importance of repentance and turning it into a constant habit.

Bibliography

Abū Dāwūd, *Sunan*, Vaduz: Thesaurus Islamicus Foundation, 2000, 2 vols.

Āmidī, ʿAlī ibn Muḥammad al-, *al-Iḥkām fī uṣūl al-aḥkām*, ed. ʿAbd al-Razzāq ʿAfīfī, Riyadh: Dār al-Ṣumayʿī li-l-Nashr wa-l-Tawzīʿ, 1424/2003, vol. 1.

ʿAsqalānī, Ibn Ḥajar al-, *al-Durar al-kāmina fī aʿyān al-miʾa al-thāmina*, Beirut: Dār al-Jīl, 1931, vol. 2.

Baghawī, Abū Muḥammad al-Ḥusayn al-, *Maṣābīḥ al-Sunna*, ed. Yūsuf ʿAbd al-Raḥmān al-Marʿashlī et al., Beirut: Dār al-Maʿrifa, 1407/1987, 4 vols.

Bayhaqī, Abū Bakr al-, *al-Madkhal ilā l-sunan al-kubrā*, ed. Muḥammad Ḍiyāʾ al-Raḥmān al-Aʿẓamī, Kuwait: Dār al-Khulafāʾ, (n.d.).

al-Bayhaqī, Abū Bakr, *al-Jāmiʿ li-shuʿab al-īmān*, ed. Mukhtār Aḥmad al-Nadwī, Riyadh: Maktabat al-Rushd, 1423/2003, vol. 9.

Bazzār, Abū Bakr Aḥmad al-, *al-Baḥr al-zakhkhār*, ed. Maḥfūẓ al-Raḥmān Zayn Allāh, Beirut: Muʾassasat ʿUlūm al-Qurʾān, 1409/1988, vol. 2.

Bedir, Mürteza, "Reason and Revelation. Abū Salama Muḥammad ibn Muḥammad al-Samarqandī (c. 4th/10th century), *Jumal uṣūl al-dīn* and Muḥammad ibn Yaḥyā al-Bushāghirī (c. 4th/10th century), *Sharḥ Jumal uṣūl al-dīn*", *Māturīdī Theology. A Bilingual Reader*, ed. Lejla Demiri, Philip Dorroll and Dale J. Correa, Tübingen: Mohr Siebeck, 2022, pp. 47-60.

Bruckmayr, Philipp, "The Spread and Persistence of Māturīdī Kalām and Underlying Dynamics", *Iran and the Caucasus*, 13 (2009), pp. 59-92.

Bukhārī, al-, *Ṣaḥīḥ*, Vaduz: Thesaurus Islamicus Foundation, 2000, 3 vols.

Correa, Dale J., "An Overview of the Current Scholarship on Māturīdī *Kalām* in Arabic, Persian and European Languages", *Māturīdī Theology. A Bilingual Reader*, ed. Lejla Demiri, Philip Dorroll and Dale J. Correa, Tübingen: Mohr Siebeck, 2022, pp. 3-13.

Demiri, Lejla, "God and Creation. ʿUbayd Allāh al-Samarqandī (d. 701/1301), *al-ʿAqīda al-rukniyya fī sharḥ lā ilāha ill Allāh Muḥammad Rasūl Allāh*", *Māturīdī Theology. A Bilingual Reader*, ed. Lejla Demiri, Philip Dorroll and Dale J. Correa, Tübingen: Mohr Siebeck, 2022, pp. 89-102.

Demiri, Lejla, Philip Dorroll and Dale J. Correa (eds.), *Māturīdī Theology. A Bilingual Reader*, Tübingen: Mohr Siebeck, 2022.

Dorroll, Philip, "Māturīdī Studies in Turkish. Historical Outline and Main Contributions", *Māturīdī Theology. A Bilingual Reader*, ed. Lejla Demiri, Philip Dorroll and Dale J. Correa, Tübingen: Mohr Siebeck, 2022, pp. 15-24.

Ghazālī, Abū Ḥāmid al-, *Sirr al-ʿālamayn wa-kashf mā fi l-dārayn*, in *Majmūʿat rasāʾil al-Imām al-Ghazālī*, ed. Ibrāhīm Amīn Muḥammad, Cairo: al-Maktaba al-Tawfīqiyya, (n.d.), pp. 478-506.

Ghazālī, Abū Ḥāmid al-, *al-Mawāʿiẓ fi l-aḥādīth al-qudsiyya*, in *Majmūʿat rasāʾil al-Imām al-Ghazālī*, ed. Ibrāhīm Amīn Muḥammad, Cairo: al-Maktaba al-Tawfīqiyya, (n.d.), pp. 608-23.

Haddad, Gibril Fouad, *The Maturidi School from Abu Hanifa to al-Kawthari*, Oldham: Beacon Books, 2021.

Ibn Ḥanbal, Aḥmad, *Musnad*, ed. Shuʿayb al-Arnaʾūṭ et al., Beirut: Muʾassasat al-Risāla, 1993-2001, 45 vols.

Ibn Mājah, *Sunan*, Vaduz: Thesaurus Islamicus Foundation, 2000.

Ibn Muqātil, Sulaymān, *Tafsīr*, ed. ʿAbd Allāh Maḥmūd Shaḥāta, Beirut: Muʾassasat al-Tārīkh al-ʿArabī, 1423/2002, vol. 3.

Ibn Taymiyya, *Epistle on Worship. Risālat Al-ʿUbūdiyya*, trans. James Pavlin, Cambridge: Islamic Texts Society, 2015.

ʿIrāqī, Abū Muḥammad ʿUthmān ibn ʿAbd Allāh ibn al-Ḥasan al-Ḥanafī al-, *al-Firaq al-muftariqa bayna ahl al-zaygh wa-l-zandaqa*, ed. Yaşar Kutluay, Ankara: Nur Matbaası, 1961.

Izutsu, Toshihiko, *Ethico-Religious Concepts in the Qurʾān*, Montreal: McGill-Queen's University Press, 2002.

Kalābādhī, Abū Bakr al-, *Kitāb al-Taʿarruf li-madhhab ahl al-taṣawwuf*, ed. Arthur John Arberry, Cairo: Maktabat al-Khānjī, 1415/1994 (1st ed. 1352/1933).

Kalābādhī, Abū Bakr al-, *The Doctrine of the Ṣūfis (Kitāb al-Taʿarruf li-madhhab ahl al-taṣawwuf)*, trans. Arthur John Arberry, Cambridge: Cambridge University Press, 1935.

Khalil, Atif, *Repentance and the Return to God.* Tawba *in Early Sufism*, Albany, NY: State University of New York, 2018.

Khaṭīb al-Baghdādī, Abū Bakr al-, *Tārīkh madīnat al-salām*, ed. Bashshār ʿAwwād Maʿrūf, Beirut: Dār al-Gharb al-Islāmī, 1422/2001, vol. 5.

Madelung, W., "Māturīdiyya", *Encyclopaedia of Islam. Second Edition*, ed. P. Bearman, Th. Bianquis, C.E. Bosworth, E. van Donzel, W.P. Heinrichs, Leiden: Brill, 1991, vol. 6, pp. 847-8.

Makkī, Abū Ṭālib al-, *Qūt al-qulūb fī muʿāmalat al-maḥbūb wa-waṣf ṭarīq al-murīd ilā maqām al-tawḥīd*, ed. Maḥmūd Ibrāhīm Muḥammad al-Raḍwānī, Cairo: Maktabat Dār al-Turāth, 1422/2001, vol. 2.

Muslim, *Ṣaḥīḥ*, Vaduz: Thesaurus Islamicus Foundation, 2000, 2 vols.

Qurṭubī, Abū ʿAbd Allāh al-, *al-Jāmiʿ li-aḥkām al-Qurʾān*, ed. ʿAbd Allāh ibn ʿAbd al-Muḥsin al-Turkī, Beirut: Muʾassasat al-Risāla, 1427/2006, vol. 1.

Qushayrī, Abū l-Qāsim ʿAbd al-Karīm al-, *al-Risāla al-qushayriyya*, ed. ʿAbd al-Ḥalīm Maḥmūd and Maḥmūd ibn al-Sharīf, Cairo: Dār al-Maʿārif, (n.d.), vol. 2.

Qushayri, Abu ʾ-l-Qasim al-, *Al-Qushayri's Epistle on Sufism*, trans. Alexander D. Knysh, Reading: Garnet Publishing, 2007.

Rāzī, Fakhr al-Dīn al-, *Maʿālim uṣūl al-dīn*, ed. Ṭāhā ʿAbd al-Raʾūf Saʿd, Beirut: Dār al-Kitāb al-ʿArabī, 1404/1984.

Ṣābūnī, Nūr al-Dīn al-, *al-Muntaqā min ʿiṣmat al-anbiyāʾ*, ed. Mehmet Bulut, Istanbul: Nashriyyāt Riʾāsat al-Shuʾūn al-Dīniyya, 2019.

Ṣafadī, Ṣalāḥ al-Dīn Khalīl ibn Aybak al-, *Aʿyān al-ʿaṣr wa-aʿwān al-naṣr*, ed. ʿAlī Abū Zayd et al., Beirut: Dār al-Fikr al-Muʿāṣir, 1418/1998, vol. 3.

Ṣafadī, Ṣalāḥ al-Dīn Khalīl ibn Aybak al-, *Kitāb al-Wāfī bi-l-wafayāt*, ed. Aḥmad al-Arnāʾūṭ and Turkī Muṣṭafā, Beirut: Dār Iḥyāʾ al-Turāth al-ʿArabī, 1420/2000, vol. 19.

Samarqandī, Rukn al-Dīn ʿUbayd Allāh ibn Muḥammad al-, *al-ʿAqīda al-rukniyya fī sharḥ lā ilāha ill Allāh Muḥammad Rasūl Allāh*, ed. Mustafa Sinanoğlu, Istanbul: İSAM, 2008.

Samarqandī, Rukn al-Dīn ʿUbayd Allāh ibn Muḥammad al-, *Jāmiʿ al-uṣūl fī bayān al-qawāʿid al-ḥanafiyya wa-l-shāfiʿiyya fī uṣūl al-fiqh*, ed. İsmet Garibullah Şimşek, Istanbul: İSAM, 2020, 2 vols.

Samarqandī, ʿUbayd Allāh al-, *Risālat al-Tawba*, ed. Lejla Demiri (present edition).

Samarqandī, ʿUbayd Allāh al-, *Risālat al-ʿUbūdiyya*, ed. Lejla Demiri (present edition).

Shihadeh, Ayman, "Al-Rāzī's Earliest *Kalām* Work. Eastern Ash'arism in the Twelfth Century", *Philosophical Theology in Islam. Later Ash'arism East and West*, ed. Ayman Shihadeh & Jan Thiele, Leiden: Brill, 2019, pp. 36-70.

Sinanoğlu, Mustafa, "Semerkandî, Ubeydullah b. Muhammed", *Türkiye Diyanet Vakfı İslam Ansiklopedisi*, Ankara: Türkiye Diyanet Vakfı, 2009, vol. 36, pp. 480-1.

Ṭabarānī, Abū l-Qāsim Sulaymān ibn Aḥmad al-, *al-Muʿjam al-kabīr*, ed. Ḥamdī 'Abd al-Majīd al-Salafī, Cairo: Maktabat Ibn Taymiyya, (n.d.), vol. 3.

Ṭabarī, Abū Jaʿfar Muḥammad ibn Jarīr al-, *Jāmiʿ al-bayān 'an ta'wīl āy al-Qur'ān*, ed. 'Abd Allāh ibn 'Abd al-Muḥsin al-Turkī, Cairo: Hijr li-l-Ṭibāʿa wa-l-Nashr wa-l-Tawzīʿ wa-l-Iʿlān, 1422/2001, vol. 15.

Taghribardī, Abū l-Maḥāsin Jamāl al-Dīn Yūsuf ibn, *al-Dalīl al-shāfī 'alā l-manhal al-ṣāfī*, ed. Fahīm Muḥammad Shaltūt, Mecca: Jāmiʿat Umm al-Qurā, [1980], vol. 1.

Thaʿālibī, Abū Manṣūr 'Abd al-Malik al-, *Khāṣṣ al-khāṣṣ*, ed. Ḥasan al-Amīn, Beirut: Dār Maktabat al-Ḥayāt, (n.d.).

Thaʿālibī, Abū Manṣūr 'Abd al-Malik al-, *Yatīmat al-dahr fī maḥāsin ahl al-'aṣr*, ed. Mufīd Muḥammad Qamīḥa, Beirut: Dār al-Kutub al-'Ilmiyya, 1403/1983, vol. 5.

Tirmidhī, al-, *Sunan*, Vaduz: Thesaurus Islamicus Foundation, 2000, 2 vols.

Tirmidhī, al-Ḥakīm al-, *Riyāḍat al-nafs*, ed. Ibrāhīm Shams al-Dīn, Beirut: Dār al-Kutub al-'Ilmiyya, 1426/2005.

Tustarī, Sahl ibn 'Abd Allāh al-, *Tafsīr al-Tustarī*, ed. Ṭāhā 'Abd al-Ra'ūf Saʿd and Saʿd Ḥasan Muḥammad 'Alī, Cairo: Dār al-Ḥaram li-l-Turāth, 1425/2004.

Tustarī, Sahl b. 'Abd Allāh al-, *Tafsīr al-Tustarī*, trans. Annabel Keeler and Ali Keeler, Louisville, KY: Fons Vitae, 2011.

Yavuz, Yusuf Şevki, "el-'Akîdetü'z-Zekiyye" [sic], *Türkiye Diyanet Vakfı İslam Ansiklopedisi*, Ankara: Türkiye Diyanet Vakfı, 1989, vol. 2, pp. 260-1.

Yavuz, Yusuf Şevki, "Mâtürîdiyye", *Türkiye Diyanet Vakfı İslam Ansiklopedisi*, Ankara: Türkiye Diyanet Vakfı, 2003, vol. 28, pp. 165-75.

Index of Qur'anic Verses

Page Numbers	Sura and Verse Numbers	Qur'anic Verses
30, 31	40:60	﴿ادْعُونِي أَسْتَجِبْ لَكُمْ إِنَّ الَّذِينَ يَسْتَكْبِرُونَ عَنْ عِبَادَتِي سَيَدْخُلُونَ جَهَنَّمَ دَاخِرِينَ﴾
22, 23	4:59	﴿أَطِيعُوا اللَّهَ وَأَطِيعُوا الرَّسُولَ وَأُولِي الْأَمْرِ مِنْكُمْ﴾
8, 50, 51, 64, 65	2:222	﴿إِنَّ اللَّهَ يُحِبُّ التَّوَّابِينَ وَيُحِبُّ الْمُتَطَهِّرِينَ﴾
9, 78, 79	1:6	﴿اهْدِنَا الصِّرَاطَ الْمُسْتَقِيمَ﴾
58, 59	4:17	﴿ثُمَّ يَتُوبُونَ مِنْ قَرِيبٍ فَأُولَئِكَ يَتُوبُ اللَّهُ عَلَيْهِمْ﴾
79, 80	7:199	﴿خُذِ الْعَفْوَ وَأْمُرْ بِالْعُرْفِ﴾
42, 43, 76, 77	11:112	﴿فَاسْتَقِمْ كَمَا أُمِرْتَ وَمَنْ تَابَ مَعَكَ وَلَا تَطْغَوْا إِنَّهُ بِمَا تَعْمَلُونَ بَصِيرٌ﴾
80, 81	3:159	﴿فَاعْفُ عَنْهُمْ وَاسْتَغْفِرْ لَهُمْ﴾
82, 83	25:70	﴿فَأُولَئِكَ يُبَدِّلُ اللَّهُ سَيِّئَاتِهِمْ حَسَنَاتٍ﴾
80, 81	42:40	﴿فَمَنْ عَفَا وَأَصْلَحَ فَأَجْرُهُ عَلَى اللَّهِ﴾
40, 41	18:110	﴿فَمَنْ كَانَ يَرْجُو لِقَاءَ رَبِّهِ فَلْيَعْمَلْ عَمَلًا صَالِحًا وَلَا يُشْرِكْ بِعِبَادَةِ رَبِّهِ أَحَدًا﴾
54, 55	99:7	﴿فَمَنْ يَعْمَلْ مِثْقَالَ ذَرَّةٍ خَيْرًا يَرَهُ﴾
72, 73	8:38	﴿قُلْ لِلَّذِينَ كَفَرُوا إِنْ يَنْتَهُوا يُغْفَرْ لَهُمْ مَا قَدْ سَلَفَ﴾
52, 53	83:14	﴿كَلَّا بَلْ رَانَ عَلَى قُلُوبِهِمْ مَا كَانُوا يَكْسِبُونَ﴾
76, 77	21:23	﴿لَا يُسْأَلُ عَمَّا يَفْعَلُ وَهُمْ يُسْأَلُونَ﴾

68, 69	9:117	﴿لَقَدْ تَابَ اللَّهُ عَلَى النَّبِيِّ وَالْمُهَاجِرِينَ وَالْأَنْصَارِ الَّذِينَ اتَّبَعُوهُ فِي سَاعَةِ الْعُسْرَةِ مِنْ بَعْدِ مَا كَادَ يَزِيغُ قُلُوبُ فَرِيقٍ مِنْهُمْ ثُمَّ تَابَ عَلَيْهِمْ إِنَّهُ بِهِمْ رَءُوفٌ رَحِيمٌ﴾
66, 67	50:33	﴿مَنْ خَشِيَ الرَّحْمَنَ بِالْغَيْبِ وَجَاءَ بِقَلْبٍ مُنِيبٍ﴾
66, 67	38:44	﴿نِعْمَ الْعَبْدُ إِنَّهُ أَوَّابٌ﴾
54, 55	9:102	﴿وَآخَرُونَ اعْتَرَفُوا بِذُنُوبِهِمْ خَلَطُوا عَمَلًا صَالِحًا وَآخَرَ سَيِّئًا عَسَى اللَّهُ أَنْ يَتُوبَ عَلَيْهِمْ إِنَّ اللَّهَ غَفُورٌ رَحِيمٌ﴾
72, 73, 80, 81	47:19	﴿وَاسْتَغْفِرْ لِذَنْبِكَ وَلِلْمُؤْمِنِينَ وَالْمُؤْمِنَاتِ﴾
26, 27	53:42	﴿وَأَنَّ إِلَى رَبِّكَ الْمُنْتَهَى﴾
80, 81	2:280	﴿وَأَنْ تَصَدَّقُوا خَيْرٌ لَكُمْ﴾
70, 71	24:31	﴿وَتُوبُوا إِلَى اللَّهِ جَمِيعًا أَيُّهَا الْمُؤْمِنُونَ لَعَلَّكُمْ تُفْلِحُونَ﴾
38, 39	57:27	﴿وَرَهْبَانِيَّةً ابْتَدَعُوهَا مَا كَتَبْنَاهَا عَلَيْهِمْ إِلَّا ابْتِغَاءَ رِضْوَانِ اللَّهِ فَمَا رَعَوْهَا حَقَّ رِعَايَتِهَا﴾
60, 61	34:52	﴿وَقَالُوا آمَنَّا بِهِ وَأَنَّى لَهُمُ التَّنَاوُشُ مِنْ مَكَانٍ بَعِيدٍ﴾
76, 77	28:70	﴿وَلَهُ الْحُكْمُ﴾
54, 55	7:8	﴿وَالْوَزْنُ يَوْمَئِذٍ الْحَقُّ فَمَنْ ثَقُلَتْ مَوَازِينُهُ فَأُولَئِكَ هُمُ الْمُفْلِحُونَ﴾
38, 39	7:176	﴿وَلَوْ شِئْنَا لَرَفَعْنَاهُ بِهَا وَلَكِنَّهُ أَخْلَدَ إِلَى الْأَرْضِ وَاتَّبَعَ هَوَاهُ فَمَثَلُهُ كَمَثَلِ الْكَلْبِ إِنْ تَحْمِلْ عَلَيْهِ يَلْهَثْ أَوْ تَتْرُكْهُ يَلْهَثْ﴾
18, 19	51:56	﴿وَمَا خَلَقْتُ الْجِنَّ وَالْإِنْسَ إِلَّا لِيَعْبُدُونِ﴾

80, 81	18:57	﴿وَمَنْ أَظْلَمُ مِمَّنْ ذُكِّرَ بِآيَاتِ رَبِّهِ فَأَعْرَضَ عَنْهَا وَنَسِيَ مَا قَدَّمَتْ يَدَاهُ﴾
66, 67	66:8	﴿يَا أَيُّهَا الَّذِينَ آمَنُوا تُوبُوا إِلَى اللَّهِ تَوْبَةً نَصُوحًا عَسَى رَبُّكُمْ أَنْ يُكَفِّرَ عَنْكُمْ سَيِّئَاتِكُمْ﴾
54, 55	4:48	﴿وَيَغْفِرُ مَا دُونَ ذَلِكَ لِمَنْ يَشَاءُ﴾
32, 33	2:183	﴿يَا أَيُّهَا الَّذِينَ آمَنُوا كُتِبَ عَلَيْكُمُ الصِّيَامُ كَمَا كُتِبَ عَلَى الَّذِينَ مِنْ قَبْلِكُمْ لَعَلَّكُمْ تَتَّقُونَ﴾
54, 55	29:21	﴿يُعَذِّبُ مَنْ يَشَاءُ وَيَرْحَمُ مَنْ يَشَاءُ﴾

Index of Hadith

Page Numbers	Source	Hadith
84, 85	Bukhārī, *Ṣaḥīḥ*; Muslim, *Ṣaḥīḥ*	احتجَّ آدم وموسى عليهما السلام، فحَجَّ آدمُ على موسى عليهما السلام
52, 53	Tirmidhī, *Sunan*; Ibn Mājah, *Sunan*	إذا أذنبَ العبدُ نُكِتَ في قلبه نكتةٌ سوداءُ، فإن تابَ صُقِل قلبُه، وإن زاد ازداد السوادُ إلى أن ران على قلبه
78, 79	Ibn Mājah, *Sunan*	اسْتَقِيمُوا ولَنْ تُحْصُوا
74, 75	Aḥmad ibn Ḥanbal, *Musnad*	الإسلامُ يَجُبُّ ما قبلَه
74, 75	Muslim, *Ṣaḥīḥ*	الإسلامُ يَهْدِمُ ما قبله، والهجرةُ تَهْدِمُ ما قبلها، والحجُّ يَهْدِمُ ما قبله
36, 37	Muslim, *Ṣaḥīḥ*	أنا أغْنَى الشُّرَكاءِ عن الشرْكِ، فمن عَمِلَ عملاً وأشْرَكَ فيه مَعِيَ غيري تَرَكْتُه وشِرْكَهُ
40, 41	Unidentified	إنّ لله تعالى ملائكةً في بعض أبواب السماوات يَرُدُّون أعمالَ المُعْجَبِين
52, 53	Muslim, *Ṣaḥīḥ*; Abū Dāwūd, *Sunan*	إنّه لَيُغانُ على قلبي، وإنّي لَأَسْتَغْفِرُ اللّٰهَ تعالى في كلّ يومٍ سبعين مرّةً

60, 61, 62, 63	Bukhārī, *Ṣaḥīḥ*; Muslim, *Ṣaḥīḥ*	أنّ واحداً في الأمم السالفة قَتَلَ تسعةً وتسعين نفساً بغير حقٍّ، فأتى راهباً فسأله أنّه: هل تُقبل توبتي إذا تبتُ؟ فقال الراهب: لا، فقتله ، ثمّ أتى راهباً آخَرَ فسأله، فقال: لا أعلم ذلك، ولكن في قريب من هذا الموضع قريتان، قريةٌ ليس فيها إلّا أهلُ التقوى يقال لها نَصْرةُ، وقريةٌ ليس فيها إلّا أهلُ المعصية يقال لها كَفْرةُ، فاقصد إلى نصرة، وأقِمْ فيها لعلَّ اللّٰه تعالى أن يرحمَك ويتوبَ عليك ببركة أهلها. فعمد إليها، فلمّا بلغ الرجلُ إلى موضعٍ هو مَنْصَف بين القريتين دنا وفاتُه، فمال إلى نحو نَصْرةَ ميلاً قليلاً ثمّ مات. فتنازع إليه ملائكةُ الرحمة وملائكةُ العذاب في قبض روحه، فقال اللّٰه تعالى: قِيسُوا واذْرَعُوا المسافةَ، فإن وجدتموه أقربَ من قرية أهل التقوى بقليل فألحقوه بهم، فقاسُوا فوجدوه أقربَ من قرية أهل التقوى بقليل فألحقوه بأهلها، وقَبِلَ اللّٰهُ تعالى توبتَه ورَحمَه
84, 85	Tustarī, *Tafsīr al-Tustarī*	بشِّر التائبين كي لا يقنطوا، وأنذر الصدّيقين كي لا يُعجَبُوا
24, 25	Ibn Mājah, *Sunan*	تَعِسَ عبدُ الدرهمِ، تَعِسَ عبدُ الخَمِيصَة
60, 61	Tirmidhī, *Sunan*; Ibn Mājah, *Sunan*	تُقبل توبةُ العبدِ إذا تاب قبل أن يُغَرْغِر
52, 53, 56, 57, 72, 73	Muslim, *Ṣaḥīḥ*	توبوا إلى اللّٰه تعالى، فإنّي أتوب إليه كلَّ يوم مائةَ مرّةٍ

70, 71	Ibn Mājah, *Sunan*	الحَجُّ عَرَفَة
74, 75	Ghazālī, *Sirr al-ʿālamayn wa-kashf mā fī l-dārayn*	حسناتُ الأبرار سيّئاتُ المقرَّبين
64, 65	Bazzār, *al-Baḥr al-zakhkhār*	خيارُكم كلّ مُفتَّنٍ توّابٍ
30, 31	Tirmidhī, *Sunan*	الدعاء مخّ العبادة
30, 31	Tirmidhī, *Sunan*	الدعاء هو العبادة
42, 43	ʿIrāqī, *al-Farq al-muftariqa bayna ahl al-zaygh wa-l-zandaqa*	دينُ الله بين الغلوّ والتقصيرِ
42, 43, 76, 77	Tirmidhī, *Sunan*	شيَّبَتْني سورة هود
32, 33	Āmidī, *al-Iḥkām fī uṣūl al-aḥkām*	عادِ نفسَك، فإنّها انْتصَبَتْ لمُعاداتي
20, 22, 23	Abū Dāwūd, *Sunan*	العظمةُ إزاري والكبرياءُ ردائي، فمن نازَعَني فيهما ألقيتُه في النار ولا أُبالي
38, 39	Abū Dāwūd, *Sunan*	لا تُشَدِّدُوا على أنفسكم فيُشَدِّدَ اللّهُ عليكم، فإنّ قوماً شَدَّدُوا على أنفسهم فشَدَّدَ اللّهُ عليهم، فتلك بَقاياهُم في الصوامِع والدِّيارات
84, 85	Sulaymān ibn Muqātil, *Tafsīr*; Bayhaqī, *al-Jāmiʿ li-shuʿab al-īmān*	لا تُعَيِّر أحداً على خطيئته، وابْك على خطِيئتك، يا ابن عمران
36, 37	Ṭabarānī, *al-Muʿjam al-kabīr*	لكلّ شيء آفة، وآفة العبادة الفترة

64, 65	Abū Dāwūd, *Sunan*; Tirmidhī, *Sunan*	ما أَصَرَّ امرؤٌ ولو عاد في اليوم سبعين مرّةً
70, 71	Ibn Mājah, *Sunan*	النَّدَمُ تَوْبةٌ
50, 51	Aḥmad ibn Ḥanbal, *Musnad*	هلْ مِن تائبٍ فَأَتُوبَ عليه
68, 69	Ibn Mājah, *Sunan*	ومَنْ تابَ، تابَ اللهُ عليه
18, 19	Ghazālī, *al-Mawāʿiẓ fī l-aḥādīth al-qudsiyya*	يا ابنَ آدم! أنا الملك الذي إذا أردتُ أمراً فأقول له كنْ فيكون، وأنا الحيُّ الذي لا يموت، فأطعني أجعلْكَ ملِكاً، إذا أردتَ أمراً فتقول له كنْ فيكون، وأجعلْكَ حيّاً لا تموت
36, 37	Qurṭubī, *al-Jāmiʿ li-aḥkām al-Qurʾān*	يقال للمُرائِي يومَ القيامة: يا غادِر، ويا خاسِر! الْتَمِسْ أَجرَك ممّن كنتَ تعملُ له!

Index

Abū Ḥanīfa 2, 3
Adam (Prophet) 85
affliction 67
Ahl al-Sunna 5, 55, 73
ʿAlī ibn Abī Ṭālib (Companion) 39, 65
almsgiving 81
al-Āmidī, Sayf al-Dīn 33
anarchy (*fitna*) 35
Anatolia 2
al-Anṣārī, Abū l-Qāsim 5
ʿaqīda (creed) 2, 3, 27, 55, 59, 65
arrogance 6, 21
ascetic 43
al-Ashʿarī, Abū l-Ḥasan 3
Ashʿarī/s 3, 4, 5
Ashʿarism 1, 5
Attribute/s of God 8, 23, 67, 69

Baghdad 1
al-Baghdādī, al-Junayd 4, 5, 29, 75, 81
al-Bazdawī, Abū l-Yusr 4
al-Bisṭāmī, Abū Yazīd 5, 25
blessing 7, 27, 33, 39, 67, 79
body 1, 6, 7, 19, 21, 33, 41, 43
Bridge 79
Bursa 3
al-Bushāghirī, Muḥammad ibn Yaḥyā 4, 67

calamity 37, 41
caliph 35
Central Asia 2
China 2
commandment 21, 77
compassion. See mercy.
compulsion 71
conceit 7, 41, 85
Creator 6, 29
creature 9, 83, 87

al-Dabbūsī, Abū Zayd 4
Damascus 1, 6
David (Prophet) 33, 85
Day of Judgement 51
deadly sin 21
death 55, 59, 61, 63, 65
deeds 27, 41, 43, 55, 57, 67, 83, 85
deficiency (*tafrīṭ*) 8, 43, 77
dervish 59
desire 23, 79
devil 45, 77
disgrace 21, 31, 69
distance 35, 55, 63, 69, 75
divine reality 23
doubt 57, 63
duty 33, 35, 53, 59

ego, self (*nafs*) 25, 33, 45, 79
Egypt 2, 6
evil 9, 27, 33, 59, 67, 73, 83, 87
excessiveness (*ifrāṭ*) 8, 43, 77

faith 17, 61, 75
Fātiḥa 9, 79
fiqh (Islamic jurisprudence) 2, 3
forgiveness 8, 51, 53, 57, 59, 63, 65, 73, 77, 81
freedom 6, 19, 21, 23

generosity 51, 87
al-Ghazālī, Abū Ḥāmid 3
al-Ghazālī, Aḥmad 3
gift 17, 27, 53
glorification 31
God 6, 7, 8, 17, 19, 21, 23, 25, 27, 29, 31, 33, 35, 37, 39, 41, 43, 45, 51, 53, 55, 57, 59, 61, 63, 65, 67, 69, 71, 73, 75, 77, 79, 81, 83, 85, 87
God-fearfulness 23, 27
goodness 9, 33, 35, 87
grave sins (*kabā'ir*) 55, 57
grief 87
guidance 17, 45, 87

habit 9, 87
hadith 4, 23, 37, 39, 41, 43, 63, 65, 71, 77, 85
Hadith of Jibrīl 21
ḥadīth qudsī 19, 33, 35, 51
ḥajj (Pilgrimage) 35, 71, 75
Ḥanafī/s 1, 2, 3, 5, 29
Ḥanbalī 6
Ḥanbalites 4
happiness 27, 53
ḥaqīqa (truth) 23, 53, 55, 57, 59, 71
heart (*qalb*) 6, 8, 19, 21, 25, 33, 39, 45, 53, 59, 67, 69, 71, 73, 75, 78, 81, 87
heaven 27, 35, 41, 51, 55, 75
Hell 27, 31
hereafter 79
holy poverty 25
human being 9, 19, 21, 23, 27, 43, 87
humility 6, 21, 31

Ibn al-Mubārak, 'Abd Allāh 5, 25
Ibn Sīnā 4
Ibn Taymiyya 6
Ibn 'Uyayna, Sufyān 85
idolatry (*shirk*) 7, 21, 29, 41
iḥsān (spiritual excellence) 21
īmān (belief) 21
inadequacy (*tafrīṭ*) 7, 43
India 2
insubordination 23
integrity (*istiqāma*) 7, 8, 9, 43, 77, 79
inward (*bāṭin*) 7, 23, 27, 33, 41, 43
Iraq 2
Islam 1, 2, 45, 67, 73, 75
islām (submission) 21
Istanbul 3
al-Iṣbahānī, Abū l-Qāsim 37

Jesus (Prophet) 35
jinn 19, 35, 83
Job (Prophet) 67
journey 7, 53, 71, 73, 81, 83
judgement 77
justice 27
al-Juwaynī, Abū l-Ma'ālī 5

Kaaba 35
Kafra 61
al-Kalābādhī, Abū Bakr al-Bukhārī 4, 5, 27, 81
kalām 2, 3, 5
Kastamonu 3
Kazakhstan 2
al-Kharrāz, Abū Sa'īd 75
Khiḍr 83
knowledge 1, 3, 23, 53, 85, 87
knowledge of certainty (*'ilm al-yaqīn*) 21

languor 7, 37
lesser sins (*ṣaghā'ir*) 55, 57, 63
liberation 23

life 1, 3, 6, 8, 25, 27, 67, 77, 83, 87
light 21
love 8, 25, 51, 65, 81, 83
love of praise 7, 37, 41
lowliness 6, 17, 21, 23, 31

madhhab 2
madrasa 1
al-Makkī, Abū Ṭālib 4, 75
al-Makkī, Ḍiyā' al-Dīn 5
al-Māturīdī, Abū Manṣūr Muḥammad 2, 4
Māturīdī/s 1, 2, 3, 5, 67
Māturīdism 1, 2
mercy 8, 27, 33, 41, 63, 69, 75
messenger 17, 41, 45, 51, 75
middle way 8, 43, 77
miracle 51
al-Miṣrī, Dhū l-Nūn 5, 23
monk 35, 43, 61
Moses (Prophet) 83, 85
Mount of Arafat (*'Arafa*) 71
Muḥammad (Prophet) 17, 25, 31, 35, 37, 39, 41, 43, 45, 51, 53, 57, 61, 65, 69, 71, 73, 75, 77, 79, 81, 85, 87
Mu'tazila 5, 55
Mu'tazilites 4, 57

narration 19, 37, 41, 75, 85
Naṣra 61, 63
nature 8, 9, 21, 53, 79, 87
nearness 69, 75
need 21, 23, 33, 39, 41, 51, 57, 73, 75, 78, 79
Nūriyya madrasa 1

obedience 23, 27, 29
offense 63, 83
ostentation 7
Ottoman 2
outward (*ẓāhir*) 7, 21, 23, 27, 41, 43

path 9, 21, 37, 39, 53, 63, 69, 73, 79
people of servanthood (*ahl al-'ubūdiyya*) 17
people of servitude (*ahl al-'ubūda*) 17
people of worship (*ahl al-'ibāda*) 17
perfection 7, 19, 23, 27, 57, 67
piety 9, 27, 87
pleasure 31, 33, 39, 79
polytheism (*shirk*) 6, 21, 29, 41
prayer (*du'ā'*) 9, 31, 33, 41, 59, 79
pride 21
prostration 81
provision 33
purification 43, 59, 78, 79

Qur'an 4, 8, 9, 27, 29, 39, 41, 43, 67, 69
al-Qushayrī, Abū l-Qāsim 21

al-Rāzī, Fakhr al-Dīn 3, 4, 5, 59
the Real (*al-Ḥaqq*) 21, 35, 41, 53, 59
reality of certainty (*ḥaqq al-yaqīn*) 21
regret 8, 59, 61, 71, 83
religion 21, 35, 43, 51
religious innovation 21
remembrance 45, 57
renunciation, holy poverty (*zuhd*) 25
repentance (*tawba*) 5, 7, 8, 9, 51, 53, 55, 57, 59, 61, 63, 65, 67, 69, 71, 73, 75, 77, 79, 81, 85, 87
responsibility (*taklīf*) 71
revelation 19, 35, 51, 81
reward 37, 81
riḍā (acceptance) 29
ritual prayer (*ṣalāt*) 31
Rumelia 2

al-Ṣābūnī, Nūr al-Dīn 67
Samarqand 1, 2
al-Samarqandī, Abū l-Layth 4
al-Samarqandī, Abū l-Qāsim al-Shahīd 4, 29
al-Samarqandī, Muḥammad ibn ʿAbd al-ʿAzīz 1
al-Samarqandī, Rukn al-Dīn ʿUbayd Allāh 1, 2, 3, 4, 5, 6, 67
al-Sarakhsī, Shams al-Aʾimma Abū Bakr 4
Satan 8, 65
scale 55
seeker 53, 55, 63, 79
self 7, 19, 27, 31, 41, 85
self-praise 7, 41
servant of God (*ʿabd*) 6, 7, 25
servanthood (*ʿubūdiyya*) 5, 6, 7, 17, 19, 21, 23, 25, 27, 29, 31, 35, 39, 45
servitude (*ʿubūda*) 6, 17, 19, 23, 31, 33
sharīʿa 29, 33, 35, 45, 71
al-Shīrāzī, Muḥammad ibn Khafīf 5, 63
sin 5, 7, 8, 9, 21, 27, 51, 53, 55, 57, 63, 65, 67, 69, 71, 73, 75, 79, 81, 83
sincerity 23, 29, 31, 35, 83
sinful act 5, 8, 27, 55, 57, 59, 63, 65, 73
sinner 8, 51, 57, 69, 73, 75, 87
soul 9, 55, 61, 63, 87
Southeast Asia 2
spirit 6, 7, 19, 33, 43
spiritual disposition (*mashrab*) 4
spiritual path 9, 73
spiritual wayfaring 53
stages 35, 43
station 19, 21, 23, 53, 55, 57, 73, 79, 83
submission 17, 67
success 29, 55, 65, 87
sufi 3, 4, 7, 21, 23, 27, 57, 75, 77, 79, 85
al-Suhrawardī, Shihāb al-Dīn 4, 5, 41, 55
Sunni 1, 5
Syria 2

tafsīr 2
Tajikistan 2
taṣawwuf 2, 37
temptation 9, 87
al-Thawrī, Sufyān 41
transgression 8, 9, 59, 87
Transoxiana (*Mā warāʾ al-nahr*) 2, 5, 67
Turkey 3
al-Tustarī, Sahl 85

ʿulamāʾ 2
umma 63
unbelief 55
Uzbekistan 2

vice 33
vision of certainty (*ʿayn al-yaqīn*) 21

al-Warrāq, Abū ʿAlī 5, 25
al-Wāsiṭī, Abū Bakr 5, 27
wayfarer 73, 77, 81, 83
wisdom 29, 33, 43, 75, 87
witnessing (*mushāhada*) 19, 59, 83
worship (*ʿibāda*) 6, 7, 17, 19, 21, 23, 27, 29, 31, 33, 35, 37, 39, 41
Worshipped One (*Maʿbūd*) 6, 7, 19, 23

Ẓāhiriyya madrasa 1
zakāt 33